BUS

1/31/05

FRIEN
OF ACPL

ALLEN COUNTY PUBLIC LIBRARY

3 1833 04803 6

P9-EGN-136

Also by Fred Brock

*Retire on Less Than You Think: The New York Times
Guide to Planning Your Financial Future*

Live Well on Less Than You Think

Live Well on
Less
Than You Think

The New York Times
GUIDE TO ACHIEVING
YOUR FINANCIAL FREEDOM

FRED BROCK

TIMES BOOKS

HENRY HOLT AND COMPANY | NEW YORK

Times Books
Henry Holt and Company, LLC
Publishers since 1866
115 West 18th Street
New York, New York 10011

Henry Holt® is a registered trademark
of Henry Holt and Company, LLC.

Copyright © 2005 by Fred Brock
All rights reserved.
Distributed in Canada by H. B. Fenn and Company Ltd.

Library of Congress Cataloging-in-Publication Data

Brock, Fred.
    Live well on less than you think : the New York times guide to
achieving your financial freedom / Fred Brock.—1st ed.
        p. cm.
    Includes index.
    ISBN 0-8050-7725-1
    EAN 978-0-8050-7725-4
    1. Finance, Personal. I. New York times. II. Title.
    HG179.B7434 2005
    332.024'01—dc22

                                    2004058087

Henry Holt books are available for special promotions and
premiums. For details contact: Director, Special Markets.

First Edition 2005

Illustrations designed by Pat Lyons

Printed in the United States of America

10 9 8 7 6 5 4 3 2 1

contents

Preface   ix

1. The Generational Pipeline   1

2. When Debt Is a Four-Letter Word   20

3. Where You Work, Where You Live   34

4. The Little Things Add Up   68

5. Insurance: What You Need, What You Don't   78

6. Education: Costs vs. Rewards   103

7. Cars: A Money Pit   116

8. The Credit Card Game   129

9. Retirement: Relax a Little   142

10. Real Freedom: Working It Out   156

Resources   163

Index   169

Cutting expenses increases income.

That simple, powerful, and often overlooked rule is the driving concept behind this book. *Live Well on Less Than You Think: The New York Times Guide to Achieving Your Financial Freedom* explores the avenues for financial survival in a society in which we are driven by consumerism and advertising to spend our money while simultaneously facing ratcheting pressure on our incomes from forces like stagnant wages and an increasing responsibility for health-care and retirement expenses. Thus we are lured into a never-ending cycle of debt as sellers of every stripe—from late-night TV infomercial hucksters to car dealers to Wall Street hype merchants—try to separate us from our money. You can, however, overcome this financial squeeze by stepping off the merry-go-round of consumption and debt to get your life in order. You can give yourself a raise—sometimes a big one—by resisting mindless consumerism and by reducing expenses. Given our vast material wealth today, cutting back doesn't require embracing a hardscrabble life of deprivation; it is possible to make big cuts in personal spending that result in only small, and usually insignificant, changes. These changes can improve your life—financially and otherwise—by freeing you from unnecessary debt and, perhaps most important, from the worry and concern about the future that usually accompany such debt and obligations.

This book is not an investment guide filled with stock picks or get-rich-easy promises; nor am I a financial adviser. Rather, it draws on the expertise of a diverse pool of experts to help chart the lifestyle changes you can make to give yourself extra money, which you will be able to invest for your future. In many ways *Live Well on Less Than You Think* is a prequel to my first book, *Retire on Less Than You Think: The New York Times Guide to Planning Your Financial Future* (Henry Holt/Times Books, 2004). That book, which was an outgrowth of the "Seniority" column that I wrote for the *New York Times* for six years, clearly demonstrates that you can retire on much less than the 70 to 80 percent of your preretirement income that the mutual fund industry or Wall Street says you need. *Live Well on Less Than You Think* winds the clock back and, using many of the same concepts in *Retire on Less Than You Think*, looks at how people in their thirties, forties, and fifties who are not ready to retire can improve their financial standing—how they can shield themselves against rising interest rates, reborn inflation, and the storm of uncertainty that is gathering around pensions, health care, and Social Security.

You *can* live well on less than you think. To update an old saying, you can have your latte and drink it too!

In the spring of 2004, I took the opportunity to follow my own advice. In May, when I turned sixty, I became eligible for early retirement from the *New York Times*. A few weeks earlier, I had been offered the R. M. Seaton Professional Journalism Chair at the A. Q. Miller School of Journalism and Mass Communications at Kansas State University in Manhattan, Kansas. After several days of soul-searching, I decided to trade one Manhattan for another.

My move to a less expensive part of the country was a strong personal confirmation of the advice presented in this book and in *Retire on Less Than You Think*.

For starters, the salary I was offered in Kansas was only $5,000 a year less than that of a teaching job I had considered applying for at a New York City university. As you will see in chapter 3, however, geography greatly affects finances. The cost-of-living index in the Kansas City area, which includes Manhattan, is 95.116—well below the national average of 100. In New York, it's 160.977. In reality, the smaller salary actually represented a raise. The cost of insurance on two cars, for example, fell to about a third of what it had been in New Jersey.

Then there's housing. I had lived in Montclair, New Jersey, a suburb that—along with other areas of the county, especially on the coasts—has seen huge increases in property values in the last decade. The profit from the sale of the New Jersey house was more than enough to allow my wife and me to buy a comparable house in Kansas free and clear. The absence of a mortgage was effectively an increase in salary. In addition, our property taxes dropped from around $9,000 to about $2,700 annually.

While the move to Kansas was a financial plus, some of our New York friends seemed to think we were falling into a black hole somewhere west of the Hudson River. I often think of them as I enjoy the pleasures of a small but active university town, ride my bicycle to work, and regard more than three cars as a traffic jam.

I would like to thank all the people who agreed to be interviewed for this book. I am especially indebted to Bert Sperling, whose invaluable data is at the heart of chapter 3, on geography and finances. Special thanks also to Robin Dennis, my always supportive editor at Holt; Vicki Haire, my talented copy editor; and Alice Martell, my wise agent.

Finally, I will always be grateful to my wife, Evelyn, for her help and encouragement.

Live Well on Less Than You Think

1

The Generational Pipeline

We travel with our own generation.
— SENATOR BOB DOLE

I spent a Saturday afternoon in Albany, New York, talking with two young couples. We were assembled around a dining room table while their three children played quietly in the adjoining living room in a three-story inner-city town house built in 1871. The house is owned by one of the couples, Corey McQuinn and Caroline Sharkey, both twenty-six years old. The other couple, Bhawin Suchak and Maureen Murphy, both thirty, live two blocks away in a similar, but smaller, house built in the 1860s.

I had been introduced to the four by Caroline's father, and I had come to Albany to get a better sense of how Generation X families were dealing with the economy. What I discovered was a sense of self-reliance that would have made Ralph Waldo Emerson proud and an entrepreneurial ability to live well on less. The two Albany couples and others like them resist mindless consumerism not by sacrifice and denial but by finding alternative, and less expensive, ways to live.

A SELF-RELIANT COMMUNITY

Corey, Caroline, Bhawin, and Maureen are part of thirty to fifty like-minded people who live in what they call an "intentional" community of lower-income people in a six-square-block area of Albany. They rely on each other for many services that most people usually pay for. Most of the children in the community attend the Albany Free School, a state-accredited alternative school that has been operating for thirty-five years. A community financial organization, called Moneygame, offers services that are part credit union and part cooperative investment group. Members pool their savings and use Moneygame's assets to make loans to each other at interest rates that are lower than commercial banks charge.

At first glance, there may seem to be strong parallels between this community and the flower-children communes of the 1960s and 1970s that were an expression of the baby boomers' youthful rejection of *their* parents' values. Yet these Gen X couples and their neighbors maintain a strong commitment to the nuclear family and individual privacy on both a personal and financial level. Unlike in a commune, they live in their own homes, regulate their own finances, and have traditional family relationships. Interestingly, as we shall see later, older boomers are beginning to embrace similar approaches—but for different reasons.

Corey and Caroline both graduated from Ithaca College in Ithaca, New York; she majored in English and history, he in archaeology. In 1998, Caroline did graduate work in medieval studies in Ireland. They moved to Albany in 1999 and got married the following year; their son was born in July 2003. Corey works for Hartgen Archaeological Associates, a company that helps builders and developers comply with historic preservation laws. Caroline works from home as a freelance grant writer and editor. Their combined income is a little more than $30,000 a year.

They bought their house in March 2003 for $33,500. It had been abandoned and needed to be totally rehabilitated. "It was a dump,"

Caroline said. They were able to do much of the rehab work with a special $27,471 second mortgage designed to give homeowners money to bring their houses up to code. They also received some loans and grants from the city to cover closing costs. Those grants and loans will be forgiven if they live in the house for ten years.

Their mortgage payment is $700 a month. In addition, they have $21,000 in student loans and $8,000 in credit card bills. They also owe $3,000 to the Moneygame, and, although their son was born at home, they owe $1,200 to a local hospital for some bills for minor complications Caroline suffered following the birth that were not covered by Corey's health insurance. They drive a 1989 Isuzu Trooper that they bought on eBay for $2,500. Their monthly expenses come very close to their monthly income of $2,500. "We're spread pretty thin for what we make," Caroline conceded.

Bhawin and Maureen's situation is similar. He has a degree in English from the State University of New York at Albany; she has a degree in political science from the University of Buffalo and has done graduate work in women's studies. They were married in 1996 and have a six-year-old son and a four-year-old daughter.

Bhawin is a teacher at the Albany Free School, where he earns $900 a month for ten months each year, a total of $9,000 a year. In the summer, he earns another $4,800 from the New York State Museum, where he works as the assistant director of a summer camp for children. Maureen is a childbirth assistant and makes between $12,000 and $18,000 a year. Their minimum combined income is $25,800 a year.

Bhawin and Maureen bought their house for $50,000 in 2001. They had been renting it since 1999, and it did not need a lot of work; they also took advantage of city loans and grants for closing costs. Their monthly mortgage payment is $450. They owe $30,000 in student loans and $3,000 in credit card bills. They own a 1994 Subaru that cost $4,300. They pay $50 a month for their children to attend the Free School and $18 a month for their children's health insurance through a state program for low-income families. Like

Corey and Caroline, their monthly expenses are close to their monthly income of a little more than $2,000.

Bhawin and Maureen have no health insurance themselves but plan to apply for it under a state program that is an extension of the one that covers their children. "In the meantime, we could get help from the Free School, which has a fund for medical emergencies for teachers," Bhawin said.

The couples' approaches to financial planning and retirement can be a bit jarring at first—especially for boomers with their sense of entitlement.

The four expressed either indifference or hostility to Social Security and even to the concept of retirement. They are not moved by projections showing that the Social Security System is sound until at least 2042 and even then, with its trust fund's surplus exhausted, will be able to pay nearly 75 percent of benefits. For them it is a distant abstraction; their formative years have taught them to expect the unexpected, to distrust projections and promises, and to count on little except themselves and their friends.

Corey pulled out his last pay stub covering two weeks and pointed out that he paid seventy-two dollars in federal income tax but eighty-two dollars in Social Security tax. "I'm cynical about Social Security, but I admit I don't know enough about how it works," he explained. "I'm cynical because of what I hear in the news and what people tell me about it. All this money comes out of my paycheck that I could be using. We're living paycheck to paycheck. This is money I could be using to buy groceries or put away in savings that I'm actually going to see."

Bhawin added: "I'm not depending on Social Security, although I'm not particularly opposed to it. My parents talk about it all the time. But we're counting on ourselves. I figure it's up to us and our families to figure out how we're going to take care of ourselves. We've got this community thing going, and I feel very much supported by it. I feel supported on a personal level, not on an abstract level of when I'm sixty-five I'll get Social Security."

Caroline said: "I'm very angry about Social Security. I think it's a bad deal. I don't think it's anything I can rely on; I don't have any trust in it. I grew up with the notion that Social Security will be gone by the time I retire. I also grew up with the notion that retirement is not a realistic option. I think that's the way a lot of my peers feel. We'll work until we drop dead. I would feel safer having the money we pay into Social Security to put into our own savings account and relying on ourselves rather than the government to pay us at some mystical age in some mystical way and in some mystical amount. I don't like something that isn't tangible, that I can't see. I don't trust it."

Attitudes like this can be found all over the Internet at Web sites devoted to Generation X. Some have calculations showing that even when Xers collect Social Security, it won't be as good a deal for them as for their parents and grandparents. This generational wedge is one of the forces behind the move to at least partly privatize Social Security.

Of course, there is a bit of the chicken-egg question here. Is the Xer approach to financial planning and retirement a lifestyle choice that will drive policy changes, or is it a reaction to policy changes that are squeezing resources? It is probably some of both.

That the Xers might be the generation that buries retirement as we have come to know it is evident in comments by Bhawin that were echoed by the others: "The traditional retirement with a pension and a 401(k) seems like a trap to me. You get into a job and spend your life planning for retirement. Meanwhile, your life is passing you by. That happened to my dad. For twenty years he was not a happy person; all he did was think of retiring; then when he retired, he decided he didn't want to be retired. Now he's working again, but part-time. I don't think I'll regret our life, that I haven't plugged away at a job for thirty years to get a pension. I think there is real instability in the status quo—in the way our society has built up these unquestioned norms like retirement and Social Security. I think it's time to start thinking of different things."

Members of Generation X tend to be much more practical and less materialistic than the boomers. Corey, Caroline, Bhawin, and Maureen are no exception. They have chosen lower-income lives and take pride in the rewards such lives offer. Rather than being wedded to a traditional career path, they have made lives for themselves by being flexible and pulling a lot of pieces together into a whole. A little here and a little there, and they seem to make things come together and work.

For most people, however, such a lower-income lifestyle is not a choice but the result of being laid off or downsized. Nevertheless, the lessons that the two couples can teach us apply to middle- and higher-income families caught in a cycle of spending and debt.

Corey, Caroline, Bhawin, and Maureen all agreed that one of the keys to their life is increasing their income by cutting expenses. "We have been trying to bring our cost of living down really low," Bhawin said. "We grow vegetables and try to have more resourcefulness in how we get things like food and energy. We want to get to the point that we don't have to have such a big income."

Caroline added: "I'm almost glad we don't make a lot of money, because I think it would get in the way. I have so much fun making ends meet the way we do. I'm proud of being resourceful. I'm proud of the way we live, of eating healthy and not watching TV and not going out to bars all the time. A night out for us is a potluck dinner. The four of us are examples of how young people are starting to go back to self-sustenance. We barter. We have work parties when our houses need repair. We don't hire contractors. We have our friends come over. We brew some beer and do it ourselves. Maureen and I have a personal trainer. He lives in the neighborhood; we cook him food in return for his services."

One of the things the conversation with the four brought into sharp focus is the divide that sometimes separates Xers from the more materialistic boomers.

Corey expressed the issue in terms of his own parents: "My parents were nineteen when they got married and twenty when they had me. My mom didn't work, and my father was a happy blue-collar mill worker who did carpentry on the side. We were a really happy family. We had just barely everything we needed; now and then we got something special. Then my dad started going to night school for computer programming. Then he made this shift to white-collar America. My mother got a job to keep up with the new lifestyle. Now my parents are getting divorced. I really think it's because of the lifestyle shift they made so suddenly; with these long-term goals, life started passing them by. I remember that we were such a happy family when we were barely making ends meet."

Bhawin remembered a friend who got a big job promotion and bought a new car. "Then he lost his job and didn't know what to do," he said. "Everything just fell out from under him. I think we've insured ourselves against that. That is the key to our lives, and it's the common thread in this community. We just haven't bought into this materialistic way of living. Half the things we had when I was growing up we didn't need. Materialism is also addictive. We're trying to teach our kids that life's not about what you have but about relationships. We have a lot of time with our kids, and that's important to me. My father worked twelve hours a day, and I really didn't have much connection with him. He's a lot happier now that he's not doing that, and the relationship between him and my mom is better than it's ever been."

Maureen agreed. "You hear people say they wish they had done so-and-so," she said. "Well, we're doing it. Maybe the boomers see us in a bad light because we've rejected their values."

While their goal is not a traditional retirement, these two couples show us ways of living well on less than you think, of increasing income by cutting expenses, and of escaping mindless consumerism.

THREE GENERATIONS

Like it or not, most of us are bound up with our own generation in more ways than we think or sometimes like to admit. As my conversation with the couples in Albany demonstrates, generational ties can have a huge impact on our financial lives because of their influence on our attitudes toward money: how we get it, how we spend it, how we save it, and how we expect to deal with it in the future. Understanding these influences can sometimes help us overcome their negatives aspects. In their seminal book, *Generations: The History of America's Future, 1584 to 2069* (William Morrow, 1992), William Strauss and Neil Howe offer a detailed look at generational issues and how they play out in our history and public policy. Theirs is *the* book on generations and a monumental achievement. For our narrower financial purposes, however, a 1997 book by J. Walker Smith and Ann Clurman, *Rocking the Ages: The Yankelovich Report on Generational Marketing* (HarperBusiness), is more germane. Smith and Clurman used consumer data to break down the business and financial attitudes of three major generational groups: the "mature," born between 1909 and 1945; the "baby boomer," 1946 to 1964; and "Generation X," 1965 to 1978. (Strauss and Howe, by contrast, include the GI generation, the silent generation, and the first boomers in the time span that Smith and Clurman assign to the mature generation.)

Smith, who is the president of Yankelovich Partners, a consumer research company based in Chapel Hill, North Carolina, said in an interview for this book that his research experience supported several common generalizations: that the matures are financially conservative and have been good savers, while their children—the baby boomers—have been better at spending than saving and are beginning to face the negative consequences of that as they approach retirement. He noted, however, that Generation Xers have more financial savvy than public perception indicates. In large part this comes as a result of learning to be increasingly responsible for their own financial futures, including retirement. The old bonds and implied contracts between employees and employers that once virtually guaranteed our futures and our retirements are continuing to unravel, as evidenced by layoffs, the hiring of temporary workers, and outsourcing. The Xers may prove to be a pivotal generation in terms of their approach to making money, saving, and retirement.

"Members of the GI generation, or the matures as we call them in our book, are an exception in American history to the extent that they have been able to rely on government to take care of their retirement," Smith said. "In fact, we could well be looking at the end of retirement, the end of this historical exception. It's an exception that has arisen worldwide, because we have social democratic countries with safety nets. But it's not the way people have historically lived. We're coming to a point where we're going to move beyond it."

The approximately 55 million members of Generation X may be the pioneers of this change.

"Right now," he continued, "we're looking at the pressure on retirement in negative ways. We can't afford Social Security; we're facing the limits of our ability as a society to fund programs like it. But when we look at the Xers, we're looking at a generation that doesn't struggle with things like that for negative reasons but dismisses them out of hand for positive reasons. Xers have grown up with a strong sense of reality and a sense that they have to take control of things for themselves. In our surveys we found a majority of Xers in their twenties were making their own plans for retirement—many more than baby boomers when they were in their twenties."

For the Xers, however, the concept of retirement is a far cry from that of their grandparents—or their parents.

It should be noted that while generational stereotypes are broadly accurate, it is, of course, wrong to generalize excessively about large groups of people. Generation is not destiny. We are all individuals, and we are all different. Dr. Robert N. Butler, president of the International Longevity Center—USA, a research organization based in New York City, has observed, for instance, that the quintessential upscale baby-boomer lifestyle often depicted in the media tends to be more pronounced on the coasts; in the center of the country, boomers are more like the rest of the population.

The Debt Jugglers

The historical exception that led to the concept of retirement started with social programs put into place in America in the 1930s and 1940s during the presidency of Franklin D. Roosevelt. Those programs led to the invention of what Smith called a "life script: work until you're sixty-five and then exit the workforce."

"The parents of the baby boomers had expectations of advantages they had earned, that they had put the time and effort into creating," he said. "They would reap the reward. Remember, for *their* parents, there was no Social Security. They were the first generation to be able to really retire in this style. It was all about the teamwork and effort of the nation at large to accomplish a lot of things. It took a national effort to dam up America's rivers and put up the power grid so that we could enjoy the conveniences of electricity. It took a national effort to win World War II. Major public works projects that we are so familiar with—the interstate highway systems, air routes, even the Internet—were created by matures and their parents. They put in what it took to realize those benefits, so it involved their generational ethic: it was about saving and deferring gratification and rewards."

That generational ethic, however, was not passed on to their children, the roughly 78 million baby boomers, whose large numbers have allowed them to remake the face of American life as they have moved through and dominated the generational pipeline.

"The matures brought up their children to enjoy the benefits of the better life they had created," Smith, who is forty-eight, continued. "Boomers have been accused of being spoiled brats, and I think that's probably an accurate description. But we were spoiled because that was what our mothers wanted us to be."

Smith said boomers grew up with a spendthrift attitude because of a number of factors, including the inflationary 1970s when people felt free to borrow money because they believed they would be paying it back with cheaper dollars. That's also when credit cards became big. But perhaps the biggest factor in shaping boomer attitudes was that the generation grew up in the context of enormous optimism about the future.

"This was the postwar generation," Smith said. "America ruled the world until the early 1970s. We thought the world was going to turn into some version of the 1964 World's Fair. It wasn't as if there weren't problems to be solved along the way—civil rights, Vietnam, the environment, to name a few. But we felt like that in every case we'd solve that problem and move on. No problem was beyond our ability to solve. We could take the future for granted; it was naturally going to be a better place when we got there. It would be monorails and hovercraft and Rosie the Robot doing all our chores for us by the time we got old. What we had to worry about was enjoying things now."

That outlook did not bode well for saving money.

"Because they thought they didn't have to worry about the future," Smith continued, "boomers were concerned about getting as much pleasure as they could out of the present. They wanted to be different from their conservative parents. So they adopted a lifestyle that wound up having significant implications for the way people manage their money. The boomers never developed the early habit of setting money aside. Instead, they learned to juggle debt, and this is something they are very good at. They grew up with credit cards and huge mortgages. They were taking out their first mortgages in the late 1970s and early 1980s in an environment of twenty percent interest rates."

A wake-up call came in 1979, which Smith called the worst year in our postwar history. "This was the year that Jimmy Carter's pollster, Pat Caddell, said that for the first time ever social scientists found that Americans held a negative view of the future: they did not think the future would be as good as the present. Polling statistics like that led Carter to make his 'national malaise' speech. This was the year of [the nuclear accident at] Three Mile Island, the Soviets in Afghanistan, American hostages in Iran, double-digit rates of inflation and interest, and high unemployment. Things seemed out of control, and Americans suddenly became atypically pessimistic about the future. My advice to people who are depressed about the present is to be glad they're not back in 1979; it was a far worse year."

Smith pointed to Ronald Reagan's 1980 White House victory as the result of his efforts to reenergize the traditional optimism of Americans in the wake of all that had culminated in 1979. "Reagan promised a 'new day' in America, and he did, in fact, reenergize our optimism. But then when we got to the end of the 1980s, when Reagan was out of office, we were confronted once again with a sluggish economy and uncertain prospects about the future. The late 1980s were really a disappointment for boomers. This was when a sense of victimization set in. We thought we had been through this in the 1970s and had figured it out. Now, in the late 1980s and early 1990s, we were suffering through the longest recession since the end of World War II and the infamous jobless recovery. Boomers came into this period with very high expectations about the future, only to have those expectations dashed with a really cold dose of reality."

Recession, mergers and acquisitions, downsizing, and outsourcing during this period took their toll on the boomer psyche. The conditions under which the boomers had grown up and entered adulthood were changing and, from their vantage point, not for the better. The boomers—spectacular spenders and consumers but poor savers—suddenly found the future less promising. "They never took any of the early warning signs at face value," Smith said. "They assumed them to be glitches that we could fix and then move on."

Boomers have always had a close identification with their jobs. As Smith put it, "Work is part of their core identity; work is a career.

You invest a large part of yourself in your career and identify with it. What you do is more than where you work. The whole concept of 'meaningful work' is something that characterized the boomer generation, boomer women in particular who marched forth in response to Betty Friedan's call to take control of their lives. By and large, the boomers' parents—the matures—viewed work in a more utilitarian way: something you did to earn a living, and then you retired and didn't look back. The boomers look for meaning in work, not just income."

This close identification with their careers is one reason the boomers have found themselves on such unsteady ground as a result of the mergers, downsizings, and layoffs in recent years. It has also made boomers' ideas about retirement different from those of their parents, who saw it as a respite from work, an endless vacation. "Surveys show that two-thirds to eighty percent of boomers plan to do some work during retirement," Smith said. "Of course, they want to change things and work more on their own terms, to do something more fulfilling. But work—career—is part of their core identity."

Smith noted that despite the boomers' lack of savings, as a group they are financially better off than their parents. How can that be? It's because of the robust increase in home values over the last couple of decades. In addition, he pointed out, many boomers benefited from the roaring stock market of the 1990s.

He quickly added, however, that the boomers' income needs will be greater than their parents' because of debt boomers have accumulated, as well as factors beyond their control like rising healthcare costs. So they still face a financial crisis in retirement. "But I'm not pessimistic about boomer prospects for the future," he said. "I don't believe all the headlines about boomers retiring in bankruptcy. Juggling debt is a boomer skill, which I don't think a lot of people understand or give boomers credit for. That ability to juggle debt will probably translate into an ability to juggle resources during retirement to make the most of them." Part of this "juggling" may involve retiring to a less expensive part of the country, which most boomers have indicated in surveys that they—unlike most of their parents—are willing to do.

Reality Versus Optimism

What was a series of unexpected setbacks for older boomers in the late 1980s and early 1990s was everyday reality for their children, the Generation Xers. These individuals, now in their twenties and thirties, grew up seeing events not as some betrayal of their expectations but simply as the way things were. They did not take the future for granted to the extent that the boomers did; in fact, Xer prospects were not optimistic across the board. The Xers grew up in a time of rising divorce rates, which climbed from 10 percent in the 1950s to more than 50 percent by 1980, and even when marriages remained intact both parents were often working. The result was a generation that enjoyed less family support than had their parents. Xers were the first latchkey kids. For support that had traditionally come from the family, the Xers turned to their circle of friends. "The Xers have always been more into connections of friends and neighbors than boomers ever were," Smith said.

"The Xers grew up with a much different set of values than the boomers," Smith continued. "Boomers never identified at an early age with values like competition and hard work. From the boomer point of view, what you needed to do was focus on values like novelty and experimentation."

Just as the boomers developed different attitudes toward work and retirement from their parents, so the Xers are following a different path from the boomers. "Xers decided that they needed to put their shoulder to the wheel and focus on competition and hard work," Smith said. "They were looking at their parents, the boomers, and seeing a whole generation of people unprepared for the uncertainty and pace of today's environment. Their parents were getting laid off by the thousands and didn't know what to do. The boomers grew up in a world that promised they would be taken care of. And it wasn't just the government making that promise. It was also the promise of corporations and technology. We were just going to ease into the future. The Xers said: 'I'm not going to grow up like that; I'm going to be more flexible. I'm also going to invest so that I'm ready if the future has a surprise.'"

Smith emphasized *invest* rather than *save* when he discussed Generation Xers. "They're not just putting money aside and thinking about some retirement lifestyle or buying property in Sun City," he said. "They are actually planning their financial future. They are very entrepreneurial about it. They see it as something they are responsible for themselves."

Smith pointed to a generational split between boomers and Xers over who is going to bear the Social Security burden down the line, a split echoed in my earlier conversation with the two Xer couples in Albany. "When the boomers say, 'We don't have enough to retire, and the government should follow through on its commitment,' the Xers reply that we should be more entrepreneurial in managing our finances and lifestyles and take responsibility for ourselves," he said. "This is a such a fundamental difference that the debate almost begins at a point where you can't resolve it."

He continued: "The late 1980s and early 1990s were a tough time for the boomers because they had the optimism of their youth for comparison. The Xers didn't view that period as great either, but they didn't see it as a fundamental betrayal of their youthful hopes and expectations. It *was* their youth. So what they developed was the savvy to deal with it: a sense of smarts tinged with an edge of skepticism.

"But, in fact, this was a generation that was coming of age quicker than the boomers ever did. Boomers probably had the longest period of adolescence in American history, especially compared with their parents, whose adolescence was cut short by World War II. The boomers stayed in college longer, got married later, and were able to act like kids for a very long time. Not so the Gen Xers. As they began to grow up, they faced the harsh reality of layoffs, declining academic standards, and a growing federal deficit. They had to learn to cope, and so they have taken more time to make careful and considered decisions about major steps in their lives. For example, the average male boomer got married for the first time at twenty-two; for women it was twenty. For the Xers, it's twenty-seven and twenty-five. By and large, people today spend their twenties as single people, which was not true for baby boomers. The Xers get involved in the life stage of household formation in their thirties."

Delaying marriage, of course, has a ripple effect on the economy and on individual finances that is yet to be fully determined. Buying a first house, having children, and starting to save are all elements of household formation affected by the delay.

Five-Year Careers

Smith and other generational experts call the Xers the generation that has developed the art of the short career. "They do something for five years and then go on to something else," he said. "Having that kind of flexibility is the defining characteristic of how Xers work. Xers don't believe in long-term commitments because—as their experience growing up and watching their parents being laid off has taught—they don't last or you can't depend on them. They want to be flexible, to be able to reinvent themselves when they have to."

A 1999 article titled "Generation X and Their Future Buying Behaviors in the Foodservice Industry," by Megan Hoffichter, Vivienne J. Wildes, and Sara C. Parks, in the *Journal of Restaurant and Foodservice Marketing,* nicely summarizes Xer characteristics. "One important lesson Generation Xers learned at an early age is to take nothing for granted," the authors write. "Life is unpredictable and full of paradox." They add: "Generation Xers have come to expect a changeable world in relation to the marketplace as well. Security is not expected. A home is not bought for a lifetime. A job is not for retirement. On the other hand, mastery is flexibility. Success is measured by continual adaptation."

Again, of course, this leads to the chicken-egg conundrum. Is the fact that fewer jobs offer defined pensions removing incentives for the Xers to stay with one job for a long time? Or is the fact that the Xers tend to move from job to job causing companies to drop defined pensions? Again, the answer is probably some of both.

In addition to reinventing themselves, Xers may reinvent retirement—or end it altogether. "Of course, how Xers retire or don't remains to be seen," Smith said. "They are only now in the stage of household formation, so their retirement is a long-term projection. But I would guess that they won't retire in the sense that we think of it today. Remember, they always want to be flexible. Given the improvements in technology we can anticipate thirty or forty years from now—improvements in medicine, for instance—I would guess they are going to have healthy, active lives that will be longer than those of the boomer or mature generations. I think Xers are going to say: 'I'm never going to retire. When I'm seventy-five, I'll probably be starting a new career. I'm healthier and I've got better technology to enable me to do that. And besides, that's the only way I've ever lived.'"

In Smith's view, people who reinvent themselves every five years or so are probably less susceptible to burnout than those who spend decades doing the same thing, and the results can be rejuvenating for society at large, both socially and financially.

Interestingly, as they approach their retirement years, the boomers are beginning to embrace some of the characteristics of Generation X, especially the connection to friends and neighbors. "Baby boomers have stressed individualism to the extreme, but there is a change now—a yearning to reconnect and reengage, with a new focus on community," Smith observed. "This helps explains the willingness of boomers to move when they retire. They are looking for different kinds of neighbors, different kinds of communities, and different kinds of living spaces. So we are seeing more interest in relocating someplace that allows people to reconnect with friends, neighbors, and even family. Leaving expensive New York City for less-expensive Tucson, for instance, is something boomers might do for financial reasons, but they are also going to be looking for a new kind of neighborhood—one that's walkable, for example—where they can be involved in a community. All these things will come together to make the boomers more willing to move. It won't just be the financial aspects, although that'll be a big part of it.

"Boomers have always been off in search of their own bliss. I often say that the only reason baby boomers are interested in reconnecting and coming back together with other people in communities is because they have discovered what medical and social scientists have always known: connections with other people are good for your health. So for the boomers, there's a selfish motive to being selfless. But, in fact, it's true. Boomers are also discovering something else social scientists have known for years: money doesn't make you happy. Beyond a certain lower-middle-class level of income, there is a zero correlation between money and happiness—and happiness is difficult to define anyway."

Another factor in changing boomer attitudes is their desire to gain control over their lives. "The boomers are a stressed-out generation," Smith continued. "They feel their lives are out of control. When they say they want simpler lives, what they really mean is they want control of their lives. Magazines like *Real Simple* are not about simplicity but about a sense of control. They show pictures of people who seem to be in control; there are rooms and settings with clean lines, and every issue has a 'to do' list in it—how to get control of your closet and so on. If the way to get control is to embrace simplicity, the boomers will do it. Those who downsize and embrace a less expensive life will do it not because it's necessarily more comfortable but because it gives them control."

Although, as Butler has pointed out, generation is not destiny, it is still an important force in our financial lives that we ignore at our peril. I have seen this in my own life and in the lives of my friends.

I belong to the so-called silent generation, sandwiched between the baby boomers and the GI generation that lived through the Great Depression and fought World War II. It's an interesting spot. I'm old enough so that as a child I learned Depression-era lessons from my parents, but I came of age in a boomer world of high expectations, easy money, and ready acceptance of debt. I'm young enough to live like a boomer but old enough to know better. Along the way I learned some valuable financial lessons—most of them the hard way.

One of the most important lessons I learned is the terrible effect of debt, especially for things with little lasting value. The ease with which the boomers have taken on debt is one of that generation's greatest weaknesses. If there is one overarching message in the subsequent chapters of this book, it is the importance of paying off debt or getting it fully under control. It is a liberating experience that can restore harmony to your life.

The second big lesson is the importance of cutting expenses to increase income. We live in a society of such material excess that reducing spending dramatically—with minimal sacrifice—is extraordinarily easy. We just need to develop armor and smarts against the commercial forces that lure us to spend our hard-earned money on the latest fad, whether it's a $19.95 gizmo on late-night TV, an overpriced vacation, a $35,000 SUV, or an identity-theft insurance policy. One way to do this is to be aware of the long-term financial consequences of overspending. Hopefully, some of the calculations in this book will be an eye-opener for readers.

In the end, how we value money says something about how we value ourselves, our labor, and our time.

2

When Debt Is a Four-Letter Word

No discipline is taught to anyone about how to use credit.
—CHRIS VIALE, PRESIDENT, CAMBRIDGE CREDIT COUNSELING

You can make hefty cuts in your expenses without the draconian measures promoted by advocates of "cheap" living. You don't have to buy used clothes at yard sales, cut your own hair, make guitar picks out of old credit cards, or reuse tea bags. What you do have to do is practice smart spending, the art of getting the most value out of your money. That will often mean looking with a skeptical eye at the "money-saving" products—especially credit cards—offered by a range of financial services companies. You also need to set up a list of priorities for spending and think long and hard about parting with your money the lower you go on the list. After all, the goal is to hang on to and save or invest as much as you can while continuing to live relatively well. Subsequent chapters will deal with various categories of spending and suggest ways to cut back.

GOOD DEBT, BAD DEBT

Chapter 8 will look specifically at credit card debt, but first we need to consider the subject of debt in general and how it can hobble your efforts to achieve financial freedom. Most financial advisers agree that there is good debt and bad debt. Good debt is money you owe on assets that are appreciating, like a house or other property. Bad debt is for things with little lasting value—like entertainment, vacations, or restaurant meals—that are often charged on credit cards. It's important not to be too hard on yourself when you have a lot of debt or to go to extremes and refuse to have any debt whatsoever. Saving money while living well may entail some types of debt—employed prudently.

Most of us, however, need to pare down our debt, especially bad debt. In recent years Americans have been living in an environment of low interest rates and easy credit, and as a result many people have taken on more debt than they should have. Although they may be able to handle it now, rising interest rates will make it much more difficult to pay down or pay off that debt. Good debt usually has a fixed rate of interest that will stay the same even if interest rates rise, and it is paid on an underlying asset that will most likely increase in value. Most home mortgages fit the bill; even many variable-rate mortgages have upward limits on rates. Automobile loans usually have fixed rates—a hallmark of good debt—but most financial advisers would consider them bad debt since the underlying asset, the car, is depreciating. Unsecured revolving debt like that related to credit cards carries interest rates that increase as interest rates in general rise; as is all too familiar to many people, the rates can also shoot up for other reasons, including a late payment. This is very bad debt indeed.

Recent figures from the Federal Reserve Board and other sources put the total amount of unsecured consumer debt at about $750 billion, or $8,900 per household; total consumer debt is more than $2 trillion (excluding home mortgages). Personal savings rates, meanwhile, have been on a downward trend in recent years as debt has increased. The amount of unsecured consumer debt per household, however, is actually much greater than $8,900, according to Chris Viale, the president and chief operating officer of Cambridge Credit Counseling, a nonprofit group based in Agawam, Massachusetts, which publishes the monthly Cambridge Consumer Credit Index survey. "The eighty-nine-hundred-dollar figure is based on the total amount of debt divided by the total number of households," he said. "The problem is, thirty percent of households do not carry any credit card debt from month to month. So if you divide the debt by a number that represents seventy percent of households, the amount of debt per household is more like fourteen thousand dollars."

A March 2004 survey by the Cambridge Consumer Credit Index shows that more than four out of ten Americans, 42 percent, were making minimum payments or no payments on their credit cards; an astounding 39 percent paid their balances in full each month, down from 43 percent in March 2003. In a similar survey in January 2004, the top New Year's resolution was getting out of debt (28 percent); it beat losing weight and exercising more (27 percent) for the first time in the history of the survey. (The Cambridge Consumer Credit Index is a monthly telephone poll of 1,000 randomly selected American consumers; it has a margin of error of plus or minus 3 percentage points.)

A June 2004 article by Mathew Ingram in the *Toronto Globe and Mail* pointed out that in both Canada and the United States, the ratio of household debt to annual disposable income is approximately 115 percent, up from 100 percent three years ago and 85 percent a decade ago. In the first quarter of 2004, household debt in the United States rose at the equivalent of an annual rate of 10.9 percent, the second fastest pace in fifteen years. Such debt has risen 30 percent since 2000.

A Matter of Interest

Household debt is a very serious problem that is likely to get worse, according to Viale. "Of the households carrying such debt month to month, one-third are behind in their payments or over their credit limits. Many are receiving penalty rates or fees because of that. These rates can be upward of thirty percent because of the usury laws in the states where many credit card companies are based. It's almost impossible for people to pay off their credit card debts with those kind of interest rates. The average household that's carrying credit card debt month to month is making in interest payments the equivalent of a car payment on a car they don't own."

The danger of higher interest rates can easily be demonstrated by using an online credit card calculator like the ones found at www.bankrate.com. Assume you owe $10,000—a little more than the household average of $8,900—your credit card company is charging an interest rate of 5 percent, you make no more charges, and your monthly payment is $200. Under those circumstances, your bill would be paid off in 57 months, or 4.75 years, and you would have paid a total of $11,400, or $1,400 in interest. At a rate of 15 percent, it would take 79 months, or almost 6.6 years; your payments would total $15,800, or $5,800 in interest. At 28 percent, the $200 monthly payment would not even cover the interest charges. Increasing the payment to $250 means the debt would be paid in 117 months, or 9.75 years; your payments would total $29,250, or $19,250 in interest! You probably don't even remember what you spent the $10,000 on. Bad debt? You bet. (Figure 1 includes these and some other interest rates.)

"Credit card debt is going to be an even bigger problem as interest rates go up, which they are doing," Viale reported. He said a lot of people have been refinancing their homes and taking out some of the equity to pay off credit cards. Using low interest rates to pay off higher-interest debt is wise, but, according to Viale, "statistics

Figure 1

The Rate Makes All the Difference

A higher interest rate on a loan or credit-card balance can make the debt much more expensive and take much longer to pay off.

Amount owed	Interest rate	Monthly payment	Months to pay	Total interest paid
$10,000	5%	$200	57	$ 1,400
$10,000	10%	$200	65	3,000
$10,000	15%	$200	79	5,800
$10,000	20%	$200	108	11,600
$10,000	28%	$250*	117	19,250

*A $200 monthly payment would not cover the interest at this rate.

show that two-thirds of households that take equity out of their homes to pay off credit cards wind up with the same amount of credit card debt within two years." He also stressed the danger of tapping home equity with an adjustable-rate equity loan: "You might get a real good rate for a couple of years, but it might not be ideal when that rate goes up five or six percentage points. In five years, the payment on these loans could double."

Viale complained that it is too easy for people to get credit: "It's so easy for people to refinance in today's world. But the problem is that there's no consumer education requirement for these lending institutions. They snap a finger and pay off your debt. Then people have their credit cards available to them again, so they build up more debt. No discipline is taught to anyone about how to use credit."

A GENERATIONAL LENS

Deena Katz is an independent financial adviser and the president of Evensky, Brown & Katz in Coral Gables, Florida. She takes a pragmatic, real-world approach to debt and, like Chris Viale, stresses the importance of using it judiciously. She is a baby boomer who, like

Walker Smith in chapter 1, views the use—and burden—of debt in terms of the different financial demands facing each generation.

"Our parents didn't know debt, other than their homes," Katz said. "But that's a good kind of debt because you're making payments and paying interest on an appreciating asset. Our parents didn't know credit cards; they saved for what they needed—not wanted—and bought it outright. Sometimes if they were known to a store in a little town they could carry a balance over for a few months, but it was not an acceptable thing to throw purchases onto a plastic card. It just wasn't a way of life, and they were not living paycheck to paycheck, which is what the boomer generation is doing."

(As Katz was making these comments to me, I had a flashback to my late father's reaction to the introduction of credit cards: he was horrified, certain they would cause people to overspend and go into debt. My mother to this day refuses to carry a credit card.)

Katz continued: "Boomers are paying for their lifestyle last week or the month before or two months before. We are the I-need-it-now generation. We don't want to wait. Life is short; eat dessert first. All these characteristics tell us: put it on a credit cards; we'll worry about how to pay it later. The government hasn't been very good at helping us out. Interest rates have been low. Boomers have seen no compelling reason to save. They have figured they may as well spend it, because they're not going to get much for saving it."

We are headed for trouble when our financial plans revolve exclusively around our present needs. "This moment in time is not what we should be trying to pay for," Katz said. "We should be trying to pay for a time when, later in life, we have to rely solely on our own resources," she said. "Bad debt can really hurt you in achieving this goal. When you're eighty or ninety years old, you're not going to be able to go out and get a job. So at a certain point, all we have is our own resources. And the government is pulling away more and more, saying it's your problem. Plus, Social Security was never designed to take care of us fully. There is a big decline in defined-benefit pensions; now, with things like 401(k) plans, it's your responsibility. But most people are not fiscally responsible when it comes to saving and investing, and that's what scares me to death with all this nonsense about privatizing Social Security. I wouldn't have a problem with it if most of us were prudent and responsible savers and investors, but we're not."

Katz acknowledged that the boomers made financial gains in the 1990s from the stock market boom and the appreciation of their homes, but she argued they could have done a lot better with those 401(k) plans if they had gotten good advice about investing. "The problem is that boomers are too short-term focused," she explained. "They panic and sell when the market is down and get greedy and buy when the market is up—just the opposite of what a good investor should do." She said many nervous investors jump in and out of the market based on information that is either old or already reflected in stock prices. "Nobody can time the market, and nobody can really educate the investor on what to expect," she continued. "Every month the media gives you a different stock tip. The truth is we have had an anomaly, fourteen years of incredible returns in the market. People got used to it, and now they can't understand why they're not getting those big returns."

This is the reason Katz suggests sticking to index funds and focusing your energy on cutting expenses rather than trying to beat the market. "Wouldn't you like to shoot par for the rest of your life?" she asked. "We're not institutions; we don't have to maximize returns. We're individual investors; we need to make just enough to get us where we're going. Most people don't know enough about investing to be making investment decisions. Index funds are wonderful because you don't have to pay attention or worry about the fund manager."

Whatever portion of your portfolio is in stocks, she recommends that it be divided among three index funds that reflect the Standard & Poor's 500-Stock Index (big companies), the Russell 2000 Index (midsize to smaller companies), and a diversified international index. She advises allocating 50 percent in the S&P index fund, 25 percent in the Russell 2000 fund, and 25 percent in an international fund—a mix that should perform very well for the average family without requiring a lot of attention or financial savvy. She does caution that having a quarter of your stock investments outside the United States could be scary for some people with a low tolerance for volatility. If it makes you nervous, she would recommend scaling back the international fund to 10 or 15 percent and dividing the rest between the other two funds.

Members of Generation X, Katz believes, are better savers and investors than the boomers because they have to be. The rise of 401(k) plans in place of traditional defined-benefit pension plans has not given them a choice. "Xers have been encouraged to do better because these 401(k) plans are all they have," she said. "They're planning for retirement, even though they expect they may work forever and never retire. Of course, it's also the pendulum swinging. The boomers wanted to be different from their parents, and the Xers want to be different from the boomers. The first thing the Xers say when talking about this is, 'I'm not going to be like my parents, scrambling around at fifty years old trying to figure out how I'm going to retire.' I see this in Xers all the time. They don't want to make the mistakes their parents made."

Echoing Walker Smith in chapter 1, she also sees Xers as more savvy about credit, especially credit cards: "They use credit cards, but they don't tend to overuse them. Once they get burned with these cards, they don't repeat the mistake. If they get into debt, they figure out how to pay it off and don't do it again. Unlike the boomers, they learn their lesson. Once they establish credit, Xers look for the best deals; they play credit cards like a game, switching from one to the other to take advantage of the best offer. I call it 'credit card roulette.' I think the Xers will mature into much more fiscally responsible people than the boomers. And as the Xers handle debt better, it may become a declining problem. But right now, it's a big problem for the boomers—for everyone, really, including the government. There aren't a lot of good role models for managing debt."

While the Xers may be smarter about credit than their parents, many of them—like the two Albany, New York, couples profiled in the previous chapter—are struggling with college loans, at an average of a little more than $20,000 a person. Even though that is "good" debt, there can easily be too much of a good thing. An article titled "The Ambition Tax" in the March 17, 2004, *Village Voice* described the problem:

> High levels of debt preclude the young from getting the sweetest mortgage deals, and they often end up in the clutches of sub-prime lenders. On average, people who had to borrow their way to a graduate degree are already behind $49,900; median debt for grad students has increased 72 percent since 1997. (Aspiring doctors have it the worst with average loans of $103,855.) Add to those obligations an investment in a humble bungalow, and you're on the hook for a quarter million or more—not counting interest.
>
> The cumulative effect is that merely keeping one's head above water, rather than getting ahead, has become the top priority for Americans between the ages of 18 and 34. Pursuing the relatively modest dream of doing better than the generation before requires serious capital—up front in the form of tuition and loans, and hidden in the form of lost opportunities. Call it the ambition tax—the money you've got to pony up if you want a college degree and a shot at middle-class bliss. But it's really more of a gamble, as there's no guarantee those tens of thousands of dollars will get you where you want to go.
>
> "The next generation is starting their economic race 50 yards behind the starting line," says Elizabeth Warren, a Harvard Law School professor and [co]author of *The Two-Income Trap*. "They've got to pay off the equivalent of one full mortgage before they make it to flat broke, in order to pay for their education. They can never get ahead of the game, because they're constantly trying to play catch-up.
>
> "And once you've got accumulated debt, the debt takes on a life of its own. It demands to be fed, and it takes that

first bite out of the paycheck. And it means the opportunity to accumulate a little, to get a little ahead, to maybe put together a down payment—it's just never there. It's just staggering to me that this is not a part of our national debate right now."

LIVING IN THE REAL WORLD

There are really two reasons for shunning new debt and paying down the debt you already have. The first is that you avoid paying interest—or, as Chris Viale of Cambridge Credit Counseling put it, paying for the equivalent of a car you don't have. The second is that a cautious approach to debt will force you to rethink purchases and eliminate many that you don't really need.

The savings can be enormous. In the final chapter, you'll be able to see a hypothetical family's savings and plug in some of your own information to see the positive consequences of reducing or eliminating bad debt and cutting back on spending. In too many cases credit card debt has been built up by buying little things we may not even remember buying when, months and years later, we struggle with a big credit card bill.

It is, however, important to be practical about debt. We need it, just as we need credit cards. Deena Katz's rule of thumb is that, in addition to debt for a house, some other debt is acceptable if you're buying something with lasting value, like a car or a refrigerator, and can't pay cash for it. "We have to live in the real world," she said. "Most people have to have a car, and most people can't pay cash for one. What you don't want to use credit for are things like restaurant meals or entertainment, things that don't last. It is not inappropriate to have some debt. Debt for college expenses is OK; it's an investment in yourself or your family. It's unrealistic to think that you can carry no debt. Most people do not get paid enough to sustain a middle-class lifestyle without taking on some debt. For one thing, having debt establishes your credit so that if you need it in an emergency, it's available. In fact, I recommend that you make sure you are developing good credit by maintaining some debt and paying it off."

Conventional wisdom holds that it is better to have a shorter mortgage or to prepay your mortgage. Katz, however, maintains that carrying a thirty-year mortgage can be a wiser strategy because as time and inflation go by, you will be repaying with cheaper dollars. "Sometimes when people get older, the first thing they do is pay off their house so they own it outright," she said. "That's not necessarily a good thing because you may be putting too much of your future into one asset." Rather than paying off your mortgage, Katz suggests putting the money into other assets.

Although Katz considers herself more realistic about debt than many financial advisers, she draws the line at borrowing money to invest. "For the average person, taking on debt to buy investments like stocks is not a good idea. The average person is just not that investment savvy. I don't encourage people to buy stocks on margin, no matter how much money they have—not in this current economic climate." In fact, because of modest inflation, coupled with generally low investment returns, you should consider paying off nonmortgage debt *before* saving or investing. "It's better right now to pay off debt because the interest on the debt is probably greater than an investment return you could get somewhere else," she explained. "This would not have been the case in the late 1970s when there was double-digit inflation—which made debt less expensive because you would be paying it off with cheaper, inflated dollars—and interest rates were hitting the high teens." But it is the case now, she emphasized, with one exception: always fund 401(k) plans and other tax-sheltered arrangements to the maximum because the money you put in them is excluded from income tax until you take it out at retirement. "This is the last best place to shelter money for the future," Katz said. "Uncle Sam is giving you a tax-free loan. You can't turn that down."

"If, however, you can invest in something that will bring a higher return than the interest you have to pay on the debt to make that investment, then you should consider it," she added. The purchase of a home usually meets that standard. However, she cautioned that when looking at the equity you can take out of a home, you should always subtract the cost of a new house. If, for instance, you own a $500,000 house, sell it, and buy a $200,000 house, Katz would count your home asset at $300,000, even if both houses were paid for. If you were planning on trading up to a $1-million home, she would not consider the first home an asset because all that money would have been used to purchase the new house. In short, equity is that part of a home's value that you will have access to after you have subtracted the cost of your *next* house. "You have to live somewhere," she said, adding that you should separate the residential value and the asset value of a home.

Get Ready for the Brewing Storm

Few doubt that the high levels of consumer debt will exacerbate our problems as inflation builds. In fact, some economists expect steep inflation to come roaring back because of swelling federal budget deficits. Other pressures are building as well—on pensions, health care costs, and Social Security. In the face of this brewing storm, getting debt under control is probably the most important action the average person can take. Katz recommended the following steps to free yourself from debt and protect yourself from rising interest rates. The suggestions related to credit cards will be explored more fully in chapter 8.

- Do not own more than two or three credit cards. Do not use department store credit cards because most of them have high interest rates.
- Try to pay off your credit card bill in full each month. If you can't, decide on a reasonable length of time to pay it off and stick with the plan. Insofar as possible, your monthly payment should be above the minimum required, perhaps one-sixth or one-quarter of the balance. Don't charge anything else until the balance is paid.

- Be alert to the interest rates on your credit cards. Learn how your credit card company works and be wary of offers, like temporary low interest rates.
- Use a bank debit card—which deducts the cost of a purchase directly from your checking account—for everyday purchases like groceries. Be aware, though, that debit cards don't carry the same legal safeguards in terms of loss and fraudulent use as credit cards.
- Avoid taking more cash out of the bank each week than you're going to need for everyday expenses. Cash in your pocket is money you'll spend.

Despite Katz's concern that the advantages of prepaying a mortgage may not outweigh the benefits of paying "cheaper" dollars on a longer mortgage, some people may simply feel more comfortable reducing their debt load by paying off their home mortgage quicker. Here are some examples of savings you can reap if you do so.

Assume you took out a $200,000, thirty-year home mortgage in April 2004 that carried a 6.5 percent interest rate. Your monthly payments would be $1,264.14. The mortgage would be paid off in 2034, and you would have paid interest totalling $255,089. However, if each month you paid an extra $200, your mortgage would be paid off nine years and two months sooner. You would save $90,076.78 in interest.

Now assume the same loan terms over fifteen years instead of thirty years. Your monthly payments would increase to $1,742.21, but the total interest you would pay would drop to $113,599—a savings of $141,490.

There is a very good mortgage calculator at www.Bloomberg.com. Go to the bottom of the site's opening page and click on "site map." Then click on "mortgage calculator." You can plug in your own numbers and get your own answers.

Remember, when you reduce expenses—including interest and debt—you increase your income. And, in the case of retirement planning, you cut the need for income. Scott Burns, a columnist for the *Dallas Morning News*, points to a Georgia State University study that shows that people who have paid off their debt by retirement need less retirement income and, thus, a smaller nest egg. How much smaller? According to the study, for each $1,000 of annual income you don't have to replace when you retire, you will need $25,000 less in your nest egg. So if you can cut your annual expenses by $10,000, you can reduce your nest-egg requirement by $250,000.

3

Where You Work, Where You Live

Clerks, salespeople, and blue collar workers
don't get paid a lot more for living in an expensive area,
which is interesting from a sociological point of view.

— BERT SPERLING, WWW.BESTPLACES.NET

For many people, where they live and work is akin to an accident—which is to say they didn't exactly plan it. They were born there, transferred there, or found a job they wanted there. Most probably don't make a decision about where they will work based on the relationship between salaries and costs of living. Occasionally, when the gap is extreme—as in Aspen, Colorado, for example—it gets media attention as local businesses face trouble hiring workers because people can't afford to live where they work. For the most part, however, people simply adjust their standard of living downward or take on extra work to accommodate higher living costs.

THE PAYOFF CAN BE BIG

Paying attention to the dramatic differences in the costs of living in different towns, cities, and regions of the country, however, can produce big payoffs in terms of your disposable income and standard of living—and the amount you are able to save. As you compare figures on low-cost and high-cost areas, you will find that salaries almost never increase enough to match your increased living costs. Bottom line: you may make more money in an expensive area, but you will actually have less disposable income and your standard of living will be lower.

While most people are unlikely to pull up stakes and move to a less expensive place, such considerations can be helpful if you are looking for a job, planning a career change, or looking for a way to retire early. We have become such a mobile society, with our families and friends scattered all over the country, that relocating is not the trauma it once was. In fact, while surveys of the GI generation several years ago showed that 80 percent of them did not want to move when they retired, current surveys of the baby boomers show that upward of 80 percent *want* to move, especially to less urban areas, when they retire. The boomers see a "downward" move as a path to a simpler, less expensive lifestyle. Such a move also dovetails nicely with the fact that they have not been good savers; a cheaper place to live will allow for a more comfortable retirement.

Even if you are in a position to consider moving to and working in a less expensive area, there are many personal reasons why you may or may not want to do so; this book addresses the financial considerations and realities. Keep in mind, of course, that certain careers may be clustered in specific cities or parts of the country; acting, advertising, and public relations, for example, tend to be concentrated in higher-cost cities like New York and Los Angeles.

Like generation, however, geography is not destiny. Just ask Matt Chiorini, twenty-nine, an actor who lives and works in Nashville,

The Relative Cost of Living in Ninety-two Metropolitan Areas

A=Cost-of-Living Index   E=Sales Salaries

B=White-Collar Salaries   F=Teacher Salaries

C=Blue-Collar Salaries   G=Nursing Salaries

D=Executive, Management,   H=Clerk Salaries

and Professional Salaries

	A	B	C	D	E	F	G	H
1. Brownsville–Harlingen–San Benito (TX)	76.249	17.50	9.72	27.29	10.47	26.16	25.17	9.64
2. Johnstown (PA)	79.709	18.83	11.73	30.70	8.88	30.68	20.60	9.90
3. Amarillo (TX)	80.258	16.48	13.60	24.05	14.88	25.64	N.A.	10.90
4. Corpus Christi (TX)	80.347	17.76	14.33	29.69	12.42	26.54	20.93	9.97
5. San Antonio (TX)	82.798	19.63	12.79	32.83	13.30	26.43	22.69	11.29
6. Youngstown–Warren (OH)	82.893	18.78	17.81	30.75	10.95	29.76	23.71	12.99
7. Springfield (MO)	83.008	17.82	15.65	28.49	12.96	24.25	20.49	9.93
8. Oklahoma City (OK)	84.295	17.07	15.34	26.13	11.29	22.87	19.18	9.66
9. Augusta–Aiken (GA, SC)	84.667	19.53	14.55	30.20	10.52	24.25	21.52	14.01
10. Hickory–Morganton–Lenoir (NC)	85.891	18.52	12.12	29.87	15.59	N.A.	20.35	11.47

11. Great Falls (MT)	86.343	17.28	14.11	24.26	11.66	N.A.	N.A.	N.A.
12. Huntsville (AL)	87.055	23.05	17.05	37.65	12.11	24.81	28.24	10.17
13. Knoxville (TN)	87.248	17.00	13.69	29.24	14.17	24.21	18.56	11.45
14. Mobile (AL)	87.281	17.00	13.46	30.33	14.55	25.68	20.76	9.31
15. Elkhart–Goshen (IN)	87.297	19.12	13.82	29.52	14.67	31.77	19.67	10.27
16. Indianapolis (IN)	87.299	20.94	16.22	30.31	19.04	28.05	23.64	12.27
17. Buffalo–Niagara Falls (NY)	87.614	21.16	17.70	35.01	13.57	32.40	22.81	12.26
18. Dayton–Springfield (OH)	87.748	20.84	16.95	32.84	11.94	30.82	22.29	11.75
19. Kalamazoo–Battle Creek (MI)	88.528	22.44	15.08	36.57	10.83	33.24	24.21	11.37
20. St. Louis (MO, IL)	89.040	21.26	17.34	34.74	11.34	30.10	21.62	12.11
21. Memphis (TN)	89.167	18.95	13.87	31.51	17.98	22.01	21.50	9.87
22. Greenville–Spartanburg–Anderson (SC)	89.435	21.00	13.15	36.48	12.34	28.27	23.80	11.34
23. Louisville (KY, IN)	89.547	19.80	16.06	29.96	N.A.	34.07	23.66	11.88
24. Tattnall County (GA)	89.620	15.36	N.A.	N.A.	N.A.	N.A.	N.A.	N.A.
25. Pittsburgh (PA)	89.974	20.05	15.67	29.90	10.64	33.71	22.53	12.26
26. Melbourne–Titusville–Palm Bay (FL)	90.440	19.71	14.89	34.03	9.25	N.A.	22.49	12.21
27. Rochester (NY)	90.465	22.07	15.61	41.51	10.30	34.62	25.09	11.49
28. York (PA)	91.252	22.53	15.64	34.86	12.79	30.80	N.A.	13.79
29. Rockford, (IL)	91.431	20.94	15.85	35.92	15.71	30.07	23.12	12.10

	A	B	C	D	E	F	G	H
30. Greensboro–Winston-Salem–High-Point [NC]	91.573	20.65	13.07	34.05	15.05	22.20	22.89	14.32
31. Houston–Galveston–Brazoria [TX]	91.833	23.18	15.13	37.16	14.46	29.05	27.36	12.97
32. Tampa–St. Petersburg–Clearwater [FL]	92.639	20.08	12.32	37.08	10.89	25.69	22.12	10.96
33. Cincinnati–Hamilton [OH, KY]	93.000	21.62	15.34	35.02	14.00	31.13	24.26	12.03
34. Green Lake County [WI]	93.357	N.A.	N.A.	N.A.	N.A.	N.A.	N.A.	N.A.
35. Grand Rapids–Muskegon–Holland [MI]	93.493	21.48	15.15	32.31	19.81	32.15	23.83	12.03
36. Clinton County [IA]	93.614	N.A.	N.A.	N.A.	N.A.	N.A.	N.A.	N.A.
37. Reading [PA]	93.848	21.61	15.29	34.01	11.69	36.11	22.56	N.A.
38. Lincoln [NE]	93.887	18.35	14.20	28.89	13.19	25.55	N.A.	10.95
39. Birmingham [AL]	93.998	19.45	13.22	30.82	10.55	27.37	21.76	11.25
40. New Orleans [LA]	94.036	19.84	14.99	29.60	12.38	25.98	23.14	9.59
41. Richmond–Petersburg [VA]	94.137	21.47	15.99	31.95	17.62	24.89	22.50	11.87
42. Visalia–Tulare–Porterville [CA]	94.149	21.31	12.01	31.46	12.05	35.20	27.21	10.72
43. Bloomington–Normal [IL]	94.404	N.A.	N.A.	N.A.	N.A.	N.A.	N.A.	N.A.
44. Bloomington [IN]	94.875	21.13	14.14	36.08	N.A.	25.53	N.A.	N.A.
45. Dallas–Fort Worth [TX]	94.990	23.16	14.21	35.63	16.05	27.43	23.67	12.37

#	Area							
46.	Norfolk–Virginia Beach–Newport News (VA, NC)	95.044	17.83	13.97	28.77	11.50	28.80	20.78	11.65
47.	Bradley County (TN)	95.060	16.55	11.82	21.95	N.A.	N.A.	N.A.	N.A.
48.	Kansas City (MO, KS)	95.116	21.19	17.27	34.70	13.03	26.95	22.91	12.82
49.	Austin–San Marcos (TX)	95.330	21.21	12.42	28.99	17.71	24.29	23.72	10.69
50.	Orlando (FL)	95.619	18.36	13.07	30.75	13.56	20.25	23.28	11.43
51.	Charlotte–Gastonia–Rock Hill (NC, SC)	95.747	21.59	14.27	33.65	17.51	23.97	25.16	11.82
52.	Columbus (OH)	95.767	20.91	14.86	38.22	13.55	31.31	24.35	12.51
53.	Greenwood County (SC)	95.771	N.A.	N.A.	N.A.	N.A.	N.A.	N.A.	N.A.
54.	Harrison County (KY)	95.800	N.A.	N.A.	N.A.	N.A.	N.A.	N.A.	N.A.
55.	Richland–Kennewick–Pasco (WA)	96.186	23.83	18.07	38.70	8.99	32.33	N.A.	N.A.
56.	Atlanta (GA)	96.613	22.91	14.91	36.36	17.61	28.94	22.02	13.29
57.	Delta County (MI)	97.238	N.A.	N.A.	N.A.	N.A.	N.A.	N.A.	N.A.
58.	Iowa City (IA)	97.665	20.69	15.45	33.87	10.23	22.03	22.58	14.20
59.	Phoenix–Mesa (AZ)	98.680	22.32	13.96	36.52	17.82	23.35	24.42	11.33
60.	Tallahassee (FL)	99.529	17.89	10.36	27.56	9.71	24.01	19.07	9.19
61.	Cleveland–Akron (OH)	99.647	22.60	15.76	36.94	16.94	31.92	23.13	14.97
62.	Charleston–North Charleston (SC)	99.962	20.26	13.93	34.47	14.53	26.87	23.62	11.14
63.	Detroit–Ann Arbor–Flint (MI)	101.539	25.33	18.78	42.91	17.17	39.36	24.85	13.42

	A	B	C	D	E	F	G	H
64. Raleigh–Durham–Chapel Hill (NC)	103.642	24.18	14.18	41.30	20.99	23.15	23.07	12.71
65. Crook County (OR)	104.025	N.A.	N.A.	N.A.	N.A.	N.A.	N.A.	N.A.
66. Springfield (MA)	104.545	22.2	15.70	29.03	10.77	35.51	24.35	13.81
67. Philadelphia–Wilmington–Atlantic City (PA, DE, NJ, MD)	105.205	24.61	17.46	38.04	17.34	34.51	27.62	14.56
68. Polk County (NC)	105.725	N.A.	N.A.	N.A.	N.A.	N.A.	N.A.	N.A.
69. Milwaukee–Racine (WI)	106.775	23.65	15.66	34.64	17.32	28.76	25.09	12.47
70. Fergus County (MT)	106.980	N.A.	N.A.	N.A.	N.A.	N.A.	N.A.	N.A.
71. Wasco County (OR)	107.943	N.A.	N.A.	N.A.	N.A.	N.A.	N.A.	N.A.
72. Miami–Fort Lauderdale (FL)	108.785	21.07	12.88	37.26	13.59	28.78	25.70	12.84
73. Portland-Salem (OR, WA)	109.693	22.59	15.97	38.49	14.15	27.64	27.03	13.26
74. Reno (NV)	111.220	19.22	15.72	29.39	13.06	N.A.	25.70	16.08
75. Hartford (CT)	113.121	26.45	15.74	41.22	16.50	39.81	26.58	14.03
76. Minneapolis–St. Paul, (MN, WI)	114.656	23.85	17.80	36.57	19.78	30.58	27.60	14.12
77. Fort Collins–Loveland (CO)	116.331	22.47	14.62	29.91	15.65	29.89	23.58	N.A.
78. Providence–Warwick–Fall River (RI, MA)	118.376	23.76	14.10	34.50	12.12	38.07	26.74	14.83
79. Anchorage (AK)	118.477	21.95	17.95	34.56	14.09	N.A.	26.83	14.09
80. Denver–Boulder–Greeley (CO)	118.946	24.51	15.31	37.55	21.45	28.42	25.01	13.82

81.	Chicago–Gary–Kenosha (IL, IN, WI)	119.797	25.42	16.93	40.61	18.77	33.46	25.28	13.98
82.	Seattle–Tacoma–Bremerton (WA)	122.978	23.18	18.40	36.41	15.49	29.46	27.46	14.60
83.	Sacramento–Yolo (CA)	123.363	22.88	16.34	33.39	16.94	36.38	28.65	13.83
84.	Washington–Baltimore (DC, MD, VA, WV)	125.425	24.05	16.35	33.74	16.25	31.93	28.25	14.20
85.	Juneau (AK)	131.950	N.A.	N.A.	N.A.	N.A.	N.A.	N.A.	N.A.
86.	Los Angeles–Riverside–Orange County (CA)	139.314	24.15	14.84	35.64	17.51	35.81	29.56	13.28
87.	Honolulu (HI)	152.731	22.25	15.99	34.64	12.66	27.87	27.63	11.40
88.	San Diego (CA)	157.650	24.30	15.61	38.56	16.54	36.78	30.16	13.28
89.	New York–Northern New Jersey–Long Island (NY, NJ, CT, PA)	160.977	27.63	17.62	43.77	17.60	39.29	30.57	14.83
90.	Boston–Worcester–Lawrence (MA, NH, ME, CT)	162.852	26.74	16.91	39.77	20.72	35.76	29.27	15.65
91.	Salinas (CA)	169.534	25.50	17.06	36.56	19.37	42.11	34.29	N.A.
92.	San Francisco–Oakland–San Jose (CA)	196.358	28.47	19.04	47.69	16.32	36.58	33.65	15.93

Tennessee, He moved there in 1999 to work for the Tennessee Repertory Theater after receiving a master of fine arts from the American Repertory Theater at Harvard University; he has continued to work for several local theater companies. "After I moved here, I never looked back," he said. "I'm working more as an actor than any of my classmates who went directly to New York or Los Angeles." He and his wife, Lynn Kasper, who is a social worker, bought a house in Nashville, and are happy with the lower cost of living. "Nashville is a fairly cosmopolitan city," he said. "At the same time, it's easy to live in and get around. It's not too big and not too small. And the lower cost of living is a big plus."

Luckily, there are some very convenient resources on the Internet that can help you sort out information on costs of living around the country. One is the free interactive Web site www.BestPlaces.net, which allows you to compare the costs of living among virtually all cities and towns in the United States. The data are among the most recent available and come from excellent sources, including federal and state governments. The other is www.RetirementLiving.com. While it deals primarily with retirement issues, it is nonetheless an excellent source for comparing taxes imposed by each state.

Bert Sperling is the chief executive of Fast Forward, the Portland, Oregon, company that runs www.BestPlaces.net. The company makes money by selling data and studies to corporations and publications like *Money* magazine that publish "Best Places" articles on where to live or retire. Sperling did an exclusive analysis for this book that looked at the costs of living in ninety-two metropolitan areas in the United States. It also compared salaries among these areas for seven occupational groups: white-collar workers; blue-collar workers; executives, managers, and professionals; sales workers; teachers; nurses; and clerks. The results appear in the accompanying table. The cost of living in each area is expressed as an index that is above or below the national average of 100, with no. 1, the Brownsville, Texas, area, being the least expensive and no. 92,

San Francisco, the most expensive. Salaries are given as hourly amounts and are based on 2002 figures—the most recent—from the Bureau of Labor Statistics.

As the table on pages 36–41 clearly shows, people generally get paid more if they live in an area with a higher cost of living. The key point to focus on, however, is that they don't get paid that much more, and certainly not in proportion to the increase in the cost of living. Let's look, for example, at a white-collar worker. In Brownsville, Texas, he or she earns $17.50 an hour. In San Francisco, the pay jumps to $28.47 an hour—an increase of 63 percent. That sounds pretty good until you look at the cost-of-living figures. The cost-of-living index for Brownsville is 76.249, about 24 percent below the national average of 100. The index for San Francisco is 196.358, nearly double the national average and approximately two and a half times higher than Brownsville. Thus, while the salary goes up 63 percent, the living costs jump approximately 150 percent. But some things, like the cost of housing, can be much greater. If you go to www.BestPlaces.net, you'll discover that the median cost of a home in San Francisco, for instance, is $560,500. In Brownsville, it's $66,900. The national average is $170,800.

The problem is the same for executives, managers, and professionals. In Brownsville, they make $27.29 an hour; in San Francisco, $47.69—an increase of about 75 percent. That still is far less than the 150 percent jump in living costs.

Using Sperling's table and www.BestPlaces.net, you can get a pretty good picture of the vast differences in the costs of living around the country. Consider, for instance, a teacher in Indianapolis, where the cost-of-living index is a little above 87. Teachers there make an average of $28.05 an hour, and the median price of a home is $111,700. That same teacher in Boston would make $35.76 an hour, an increase of 27 percent. The cost-of-living index for Boston, though, is 162.852, almost double that for Indianapolis, and the median cost of a house in Boston is $316,900. In some trendy suburbs the median can climb above $500,000; in Brookline, for instance, it's $984,800. Which teacher is going to have more disposable income? Which teacher is going to be able to save and invest more?

Sperling, who is the coauthor of *Cities Ranked and Rated: More than 400 Metropolitan Areas Evaluated in the U.S. and Canada* (John Wiley & Sons, 2004), pointed out that the data he put together for this book do not take taxes into account. If you move to a more expensive area and get a raise, you will presumably have to pay more income taxes, which would reduce your disposable income even further. Moreover, state and local taxes would also tend to be higher.

Tom Wetzel, the president of the Retirement Living Information Center, which operates the www.RetirementLiving.com site, says that because of the wide variations in property taxes, it is very difficult to come to a definitive conclusion about which states are the most and least expensive. His Web site, however, contains a ranking of states according to the total tax burden, expressed as a percentage of income. The data come from the Census Bureau and include local property taxes, sales taxes, income taxes, and so on. They do not include any federal taxes, but they do take into account local and state taxes on businesses. This ranking is probably more valuable for the average person than, say, a ranking of taxes paid on a per-capita basis because of distortions from widely varying populations and incomes among the states.

According to the www.RetirementLiving.com list, the five states with the highest state and local tax burden are as a percentage of income are: New York (12.9 percent), Maine (12.3 percent), Ohio (11.3 percent), Hawaii (11.3 percent), and Rhode Island (tied with Wisconsin at 11.1 percent). The national average is 10 percent; the District of Columbia is 12.8 percent.

The lowest five states are: Alaska (6.3 percent), New Hampshire (7.5 percent), Delaware (8.2 percent), Tennessee (8.5 percent), and Texas (8.7 percent).

Here's the complete list:

New York (12.9 percent)
Maine (12.3 percent)
Ohio (11.3 percent)
Hawaii (11.3 percent)
Rhode Island (11.1 percent)
Wisconsin (11.1 percent)
Utah (10.8 percent)
Connecticut (10.6 percent)
West Virginia (10.6 percent)
Minnesota (10.5 percent)
Idaho (10.4 percent)
Vermont (10.4 percent)
Michigan (10.2 percent)
Nebraska (10.2 percent)
New Jersey (10.1 percent)
Indiana (10.1 percent)
Arizona (10.0 percent)
Georgia (10.0 percent)
Kentucky (10.0 percent)
Mississippi (10.0 percent)
Kansas (9.9 percent)
Louisiana (9.9 percent)
Maryland (9.9 percent)
Washington (9.9 percent)
Arkansas (9.8 percent)
California (9.8 percent)
Iowa (9.8 percent)
Montana (9.8 percent)
Illinois (9.7 percent)
New Mexico (9.7 percent)
Nevada (9.7 percent)
North Carolina (9.7 percent)
North Dakota (9.7 percent)
Oregon (9.5 percent)

Massachusetts (9.4 percent)

Pennsylvania (9.4 percent)

Missouri (9.3 percent)

Virginia (9.3 percent)

Oklahoma (9.2 percent)

Alabama (9.1 percent)

Colorado (9.1 percent)

South Carolina (9.0 percent)

South Dakota (9.0 percent)

Wyoming (8.9 percent)

Florida (8.8 percent)

Texas (8.7 percent)

Tennessee (8.5 percent)

Delaware (8.2 percent)

New Hampshire (7.5 percent)

Alaska (6.3 percent)

You can do your own calculations using different cities and occupational groups and find that in virtually every case there is a financial penalty for moving to a more expensive area; conversely, there is a financial reward for doing the opposite. At www.Best Places.net, you can also plug in your salary and see how much more or less it would take to maintain a comparable lifestyle in another city or town.

"These data show what one would expect," Sperling said of the table he created for this book. "Where there is a lower cost of living, there are lower salaries; where there are higher costs, there are higher salaries. However, no occupational group is financially better off in a more expensive area, although white-collar workers and professionals make out better than some other groups. Clerks, salespeople, and blue-collar workers don't get paid a lot more for living in an expensive area, which is interesting from a sociological point of view.

"If people were making a job decision solely based on money, they would not pick an expensive area like San Francisco. If they were trying to maximize their earnings, they would take a lower salary in a less expensive area instead of a high salary in a more expensive place." For someone doing career planning or contemplating a career change, that's worth considering.

Sperling prepared data for the accompanying three graphs to better illustrate these points. In all three, the hourly pay rate is on the left and the cost-of-living index is at the bottom. Each graph contains two trends lines for two occupational groups. In figure 2, the top trend line is for white-collar workers and the bottom trend line for blue-collar workers. The trend lines in all three graphs begin with hourly pay in Brownsville and advance to San Francisco. The flatter the trend line, the greater a worker is financially hurt by moving to a more expensive area. If a trend line were at a forty-five-degree angle, which none is, it would mean pay would be rising exactly in tandem with living costs. As figure 2 clearly shows, blue-collar workers do not make out as well as their white-collar counterparts. Figure 3 shows similar results for executives, managers, and professionals (top trend line) and sales workers (bottom trend line). Figure 4 reflects data for nurses and clerks.

From the Coast to the Heartland

Let's apply some of these statistics to a hypothetical couple, John and Jane Doe, who live in White Plains, New York, a northern suburb of New York City. They are in their mid-forties and have a daughter and a son in college. John is an accountant who commutes each day to his office in New York. Jane is a nurse and works at a local hospital. Using Sperling's data and assuming a thirty-five-hour workweek, we see that John earns $43.77 an hour, or $79,661.40 a year; Jane makes $30.57 an hour, or $55,637.40 a year. This gives the couple a combined annual income of $135,298.80. They live, however, in one of the most expensive areas in the country and wonder if they would be better off in a cheaper place, even if they made less money. After all, they have another twenty years of work ahead of them. They also have grown weary of the traffic and congestion in

Figure 2

Incomes and the Cost of Living

Though jobs tend to pay more in expensive communities, the difference is usually not as great as the difference in the cost of living, making workers there worse off despite the higher pay. The effect is especially severe for blue-collar workers.

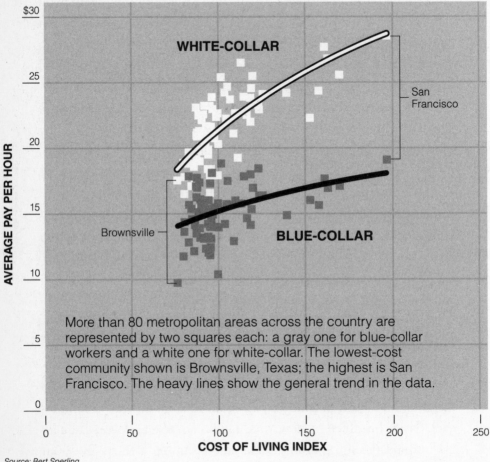

More than 80 metropolitan areas across the country are represented by two squares each: a gray one for blue-collar workers and a white one for white-collar. The lowest-cost community shown is Brownsville, Texas; the highest is San Francisco. The heavy lines show the general trend in the data.

Source: Bert Sperling

the New York metropolitan area. From road trips they have taken around the country, they have become fond of some less crowded areas in the lower Midwest. They like certain aspects of the South but also enjoy cold-weather activities and four distinct seasons.

After some research, they decide to take a closer look at Madi-

Figure 3

Higher on the Totem Pole

For executives and managers, the higher pay available in a high cost-of-living community may or may not be enough to compensate for added costs. But for salespeople, pay tends to be only slightly higher in expensive communties.

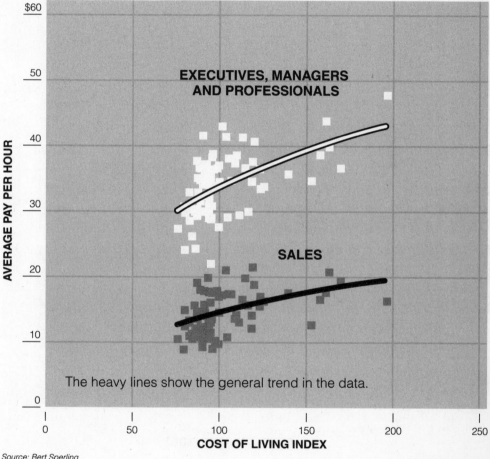

Source: Bert Sperling

son, a small town in southern Indiana. They have visited Madison twice in the past because Jane has a cousin who is a high school teacher there. Employment prospects look promising: there are job openings for nurses at the local hospital, as well as for accountants at several small manufacturing companies in the area.

Figure 4

Parity and Geography

On average, nurses are paid significantly more in communities where the cost of living is high than where it is low, but clerks' earnings vary much less from community to community.

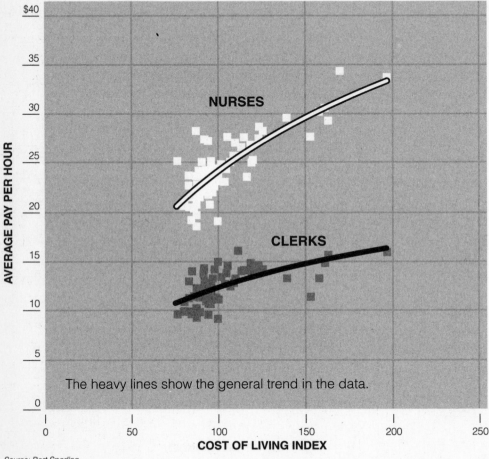

The heavy lines show the general trend in the data.

Source: Bert Sperling

What would such a move mean for their finances? According to the Sperling data—using figures for Louisville, Kentucky, the nearest metropolitan area—John could expect to make $29.96 an hour, or $54,527.20 a year, in Madison; Jane could expect $23.66 an hour, or $43,061.20 a year. Their combined Madison income would be

$97,588.40, which is about 28 percent, or $37,710.40, less than they make in New York. At first John and Jane are put off by such a cut in salary.

Then they compare the costs of living.

The Louisville and southern Indiana area is the twenty-third cheapest in the country, with a cost-of-living index of 89.547, compared with the national average of 100 and the New York City metropolitan area's index of 160.977, making it the fourth most expensive region of the United States. This means it costs almost 45 percent less to live in Madison than in White Plains. Or, put another way, if you make $100,000 a year in New York, you can have a comparable lifestyle in Madison for $55,000 a year. That makes a 28 percent salary cut look pretty sweet. If we use data for Cincinnati, Ohio, the second closest city to Madison, the results are similar. Cincinnati is the thirty-third least expensive metropolitan area, with a cost-of-living index of 93.000—42 percent less than that for New York.

A big part of the difference in the costs of living is housing. The median value of a home in White Plains is $577,300. In Madison, it's $105,600, well below the national average of $170,800.

In many ways, Madison is ideal for a couple like John and Jane, who are looking not only for a place where their incomes will go farther but also for a simpler life in a less populated place.

Located on the Ohio River in a bucolic setting, Madison is a historic, self-contained town of 13,000 that is not a suburban bedroom community for a larger city. Additionally, it's not an exit town for an interstate highway, although interstate access is available a few miles to the east (I-65) and to the south (I-71) in Kentucky. Madison, however, is far from isolated: nearby Hanover College lends an academic flavor; Louisville is less than an hour away; Cincinnati and Indianapolis are less than two hours away, as is Bloomington, the home of Indiana University and a town cited as a top retirement spot on many "best places" lists.

While Madison itself has several good restaurants and plenty of activities throughout the year, its proximity to these larger cities means easy access to the cultural and sporting activities they offer, as well as a broader range of restaurants and retail stores. And even though Madison has plenty of doctors and a good, small hospital where Jane expects to work, it's comforting for the couple to know that they are close to the top-flight medical care and range of medical specialties available in these larger cities.

John and Jane like history, and Madison is a history buff's paradise—a nineteenth-century time capsule. As one longtime resident puts it: "I always tell people that Madison is the kind of town where, if Mark Twain were to return, he would feel right at home. Especially when the *Delta Queen* comes paddle-wheeling down from Cincinnati." The central downtown Historic District, with its church spires and striking architecture, is a beautifully preserved example of early- and middle-nineteenth-century Americana. It's sometimes referred to as a midwestern version of Charleston, South Carolina. John and Jane first became aware of Madison when they saw the 1958 film *Some Came Running*, which was filmed there and stars Frank Sinatra, Dean Martin, and Shirley MacLaine. The movie, based on the novel by James Jones, includes long, lingering shots of Madison's buildings and vistas.

The town's activities throughout the year include the Madison Regatta in July, which features 200-mile-an-hour hydroplane racing on the Ohio River; a balloon race; the Chautauqua arts and crafts festival; and various Christmas programs. Nearby Hanover College also has a full program of speakers and events open to the public. Every Saturday morning during the summer and fall there's a farmers market on the courthouse square. Traffic and parking problems seldom occur; there aren't even any parking meters.

The town is surrounded by the rolling countryside of southern Indiana. The state's image as an unbroken flat landscape comes from the fact that most people see it from Interstate 70, which cuts east-west through the center of the state, or from Interstate 80 along the Michigan border. The northern two-thirds of the state is indeed mostly flat, the result of prehistoric glaciers. In contrast, the southern third, where Madison is located, has plenty of wooded hills that fan out to the south and the Ohio River.

It is that geography that gave Madison's two distinct sections their local names: "downtown" and "the hilltop." Downtown refers to the mainly historic section along the river, including a wide, brick-lined riverfront promenade. The hilltop—accessible by three steep, scenic roads—is the newer and more commercial part of town. It's home to the usual retail stores, auto dealers, and subdivisions. From the hilltop there are spectacular views of downtown and the Ohio River valley.

To be content in Madison, John and Jane would have to adjust to the pace of living in a small town. But because it's close, but not too close, to three big cities, they can have the best of both as they wish.

WHO'LL SIT AT THE BOOMERS' DESKS?

If you're looking for a job or considering changing jobs—and perhaps using the opportunity to move to a less expensive place—there are some optimistic signs you should be aware of.

Remember during the boom years of the late 1990s when employees were in short supply and corporations were struggling to hire and retain workers? One recession and one mostly jobless recovery later, workers could be excused for wondering if that period was a temporary golden moment for American workers. Was the worker shortage an anomaly? Will relatively high unemployment be the norm for the near future?

The answers appear to be no and no.

In fact, conditions in the late 1990s may have been a reflection of job markets to come, and they are coming very quickly. The reason, of course, is that the big baby-boom generation is starting to retire. As of this writing, its oldest members are about fifty-eight, and will be sixty-five in 2011. There simply aren't enough workers behind the boomers to fill their jobs. Employers will be competing fiercely for workers, a development likely to push up salaries. It will also be good for retirees who want to continue working in some capacity.

Many companies are woefully unprepared to cope with this demographic development. "It's stunning how many corporations and chief executives have no idea what's coming; they're so focused on their next quarter's numbers," said Paul Kaihla, a senior writer for the magazine *Business 2.0*, a Time Inc. publication, for which he wrote a cover story, "The Coming Job Boom," in September 2003. He called the situation a "retirement time bomb" that will gut the ranks of management and skilled workers, particularly in the technology sector.

In fact, this labor crisis is looming now, as some boomers take early retirement. These early retirees, according to Kaihla, are actually shaving a couple of percentage points off the unemployment rate. "The labor shortage has been masked by recession," he said. "By 2005 it should be in full swing. By 2010 there will be a gap of five million to seven million workers, depending on whose projections you accept." Some projections show that gap swelling to a canyon of 14 million workers by 2020, he reported.

"You can't have the vast majority of your prime-age workforce retire and not have it have an effect," Kaihla continued. "Always before, the generation coming in was larger than the previous one. That's not the case now. The feeder pool isn't providing the kind of natural growth we've always had in the workforce."

He also noted that the rate of higher education among workers has leveled off at about 60 percent—meaning that share of workers has some college education. "This is likely to get only marginally higher," he added.

Nowhere is the potential worker shortage more pronounced, Kaihla said, than at federal agencies like the Defense Department, where half the current civilian workers are scheduled to retire by 2010. He predicted that the coming labor shortage will put an end to outsourcing as a contentious labor issue, and that Congress will increase the number of skilled workers allowed into the country.

While this is all good news for workers, the downside, in Kaihla's view, is that we may face slower economic growth if companies can't hire enough workers.

Some economists, however, aren't so sure. Henry J. Aaron and Gary Burtless, senior fellows at the Brookings Institution in Washington, D.C., cited the flexibility of the American workforce as a factor that may soften the effects of boomers' retirements. "Workers may take higher-level jobs at a younger age than we have traditionally seen," Burtless said. Both agreed, though, that the leveling off of the education rate among workers could be a problem as employers try to fill positions for skilled workers and managers.

According to Beverly Goldberg, a vice president of the Century Foundation, a research institute in New York, the projections for labor shortages are likely to be pretty much on target since "demographics don't change." Goldberg, who is also the author of *Age Works: What Corporations Must Do to Survive the Graying of the Work Force* (Free Press, 2002), noted that Europe would have more difficulty dealing with labor shortages than the United States because of more restrictive immigration policies and lower birth rates. She added, however, that one problem in trying to import workers is that they often lack the necessary skills to replace older workers. She said the shortage was already painfully evident in occupations like teaching, where people often retire after thirty years: "Teachers are retiring in astounding numbers. New York City is combing the world looking for teachers." Nevertheless, "more companies than not are lulled into a false sense of security. They have to face the fact that they're next."

Added Kaihla: "There has never been a clear example in modern economic times of what we are facing."

Where the Jobs Will Be

In the March 2004 issue of *Business 2.0*, Kaihla wrote an article in which he ranked the top twenty boomtowns or metropolitan areas in America in terms of jobs that will be created by 2008. At the top of the list was Raleigh-Durham, North Carolina. Note, however, that on Bert Sperling's cost-of-living ranking that appears earlier in this chapter, Raleigh-Durham came in at no. 64 (with 92 being the most expensive), with a cost-of-living index of 103.642 (compared with the national average of 100). Phoenix ranked twelfth on Kaihla's list and fifty-ninth on Sperling's, with a cost-of-living index of 98.680. Clearly, there are jobs to be had in less expensive areas. Following is Kaihla's complete list from which you can make your own comparison with Sperling's list. Because the lists are based on different data, not all town names appear on both lists. You may have to use figures on the Sperling list for another town in the general area or go to www.BestPlaces.net for a more exact comparison.

Raleigh–Durham, North Carolina
San Jose, California
Washington, D.C.
Austin, Texas
Atlanta, Georgia
West Palm Beach, Florida
San Francisco–Oakland, California
Middlesex–Somerset, New Jersey
Seattle, Washington
Boston, Massachusetts
Sacramento, California
Phoenix, Arizona
Minneapolis, Minnesota
Denver, Colorado
New Haven–Stamford, Connecticut
Baltimore, Maryland

San Diego, California
Dallas, Texas
Charlotte, North Carolina
Philadelphia, Pennsylvania

Kaihla singled out ten smaller towns where job growth is also expected to be robust, but the pace of life is slower:

Boulder, Colorado
Fort Collins, Colorado
Santa Fe, New Mexico
Charlottesville, Virginia
Boise, Idaho
Colorado Springs, Colorado
Gainesville, Florida
Trenton, New Jersey
Tallahassee, Florida
Olympia, Washington

Keep in mind that even though an area may be expensive, there are often nearby towns that are less so. But, of course, you then have to budget for increased commuting expenses.

MORE THAN A HOME

For most people, a home is their biggest single expense. It is also likely to be their biggest source of savings and investment. Home prices have been rising at a fast clip in the last few years, especially on the East and West Coasts. Many people who bought their houses a decade or so ago find themselves living in homes they could not afford if they had to buy them today. This is especially true of desirable areas in and around expensive cities and puts an extra burden on first-time home buyers. The rising prices have been pushed by low interest rates that have kept monthly payments down and by adjustable-rate mortgages that carry very low initial rates. Some economists see a housing market bubble ready to burst as rates rise; others think the market might take a hit, but only in the areas where it has been red-hot. Still others expect it to continue its upward climb, at least until the baby boomers start to retire and begin migrating out of the big cities. That, of course, will in turn increase prices wherever these retirees, flush with money from the sales of their homes, end up. Remember, however, that the boomers are a twenty-year phenomenon working through the system; the changes they cause in the housing market will probably be gradual and less disruptive than many fear. They're not going to all sell their houses as soon as they retire any more than they're going to suddenly pull all their money out of the stock market.

In fact, a gradual easing of the growth in home prices might be a good thing overall. One result of the housing boom is that many people have simply been priced of the market in places like New York and San Francisco. A recent article in the *New York Times* cited potential buyers simply giving up in the face of average sales prices for Manhattan apartments that were approaching $1 million. The monthly payments on a thirty-year mortgage for $1 million at a rate of 6.5 percent would be $6,320. A $750,000 mortgage would mean payments of $4,740 a month. These figures don't include taxes and other expenses like condo fees or co-op maintenance charges. With prices like these, paying $2,000 a month for rent might not look so bad.

The reality, however, is that renting—and building no equity in a home—is unlikely to be a money-saving move in the long run. Of course, in the short term the increase in housing prices could ease, and prices could even decline in some cases. Over the long haul, however, it's hard to make a case against home ownership. Mortgage interest, which is most of a mortgage payment for many years, and property taxes are deductible from your income taxes; rent is not. If you buy and have a fixed-rate mortgage, you have stabilized most of your housing costs no matter what happens to inflation and the rental market. Your house, in which you are building equity, is almost certain to increase in value over the years; rent builds no equity. Even if the home you buy doesn't rise in value as rapidly as in the past or as property in more desirable areas, you'll still be better off than having paid rent. What all this means in the end is that when you retire, you'll probably be able to sell your home and use the profit to buy another one mortgage-free in a less expensive area. Not so if you have been renting.

I'm not advocating you buy a $1-million apartment. Go where you can afford to buy, even if that means a longer commute. You may even have to stretch yourself a bit financially for a few years, but that's OK because you're putting money into an appreciating asset—the very definition of good debt. A portion of your living expenses becomes part of your investment portfolio. If you use savings from cutting expenses in other parts of your budget to help with a mortgage payment, so much the better. You are basically using day-to-day savings to increase long-term savings. Most people are unlikely to get a rate of return for their money that beats the long-term appreciation on their home, especially given that it's an investment you can live in.

We can't predict the future, but we can look at the past. The Office of Federal Housing Enterprise Oversight (OFHEO), a government agency that tracks changes in home values, has a Web site (www.ofheo.gov) with all kinds of data on home prices around the United States. From April 1, 2003 through March 31, 2004, prices increased an average of 7.71 percent, although they slowed to an annual rate of 3.84 percent in the final quarter of that period. Six states—Vermont, Alaska, North Dakota, South Dakota, Iowa, and Nebraska—actually showed slight declines in home prices for that last quarter. In a statement, Patrick Lawler, the chief economist at OFHEO, praised the slowing in the final quarter because he said continued big price jumps "would raise the potential for declines later on."

As might be expected from Bert Sperling's data, the annual increases varied widely from state to state and from city to city, with growth in some areas that was double the national average. From highest to lowest, here's the annual rise in home prices in the states and the District of Columbia; the second list of percentages is for the last five years, and the third is the total increase since 1980.

State	1-Year	5-Year	Since 1980
Hawaii	15.16	43.98	236.60
Nevada	15.08	40.37	160.79
Rhode Island	14.80	80.24	361.36
Washington, D.C.	14.33	92.96	302.84
California	13.94	76.97	314.95
Maryland	12.87	52.26	245.90
Florida	11.67	55.42	195.57
New Jersey	10.93	61.82	315.63
Delaware	10.38	44.61	265.53
New York	10.23	61.36	398.79
Virginia	10.12	48.66	223.63
Maine	9.86	56.68	302.32
Vermont	9.78	43.84	238.71
Massachusetts	9.29	75.50	516.30
Montana	9.16	32.41	170.25
Connecticut	9.10	50.49	273.03
New Hampshire	9.00	71.33	307.20
Minnesota	8.04	56.18	216.43
UNITED STATES	**7.71**	**41.73**	**209.60**
Pennsylvania	7.65	32.86	206.89
Alaska	7.40	24.80	103.72
Arizona	7.19	34.78	152.85
Wyoming	6.58	31.40	93.22
Illinois	6.39	33.54	201.72
Wisconsin	6.01	29.86	172.41
Oregon	5.91	24.72	202.92

New Mexico	5.89	19.51	138.92
Washington	5.77	29.43	228.77
North Dakota	5.61	21.84	96.35
Missouri	5.30	30.82	156.10
Arkansas	4.86	20.70	116.07
West Virginia	4.82	20.68	100.06
South Dakota	4.57	24.46	135.12
Oklahoma	4.47	24.00	73.91
Iowa	4.45	22.90	120.76
Louisiana	4.43	24.38	92.11
Kentucky	4.29	22.77	157.52
South Carolina	4.01	24.81	116.67
Georgia	3.96	30.25	184.12
Idaho	3.94	18.61	136.88
Kansas	3.88	25.67	114.68
Michigan	3.75	29.28	202.55
Ohio	3.73	21.28	154.63
Nebraska	3.62	19.43	129.16
North Carolina	3.44	21.14	177.93
Mississippi	3.36	19.15	110.86
Tennessee	3.32	18.38	150.87
Alabama	3.18	19.67	134.49
Colorado	2.85	40.54	223.93
Indiana	2.80	18.01	137.09
Texas	2.34	26.03	88.60
Utah	1.95	9.98	162.56

As the above list indicates, some regions have done better than others in terms of rising home prices. OFHEO uses nine regional divisions created by the U.S. Census Bureau (see figure 5).

Figure 5

U.S. Census Divisions

Pacific
Alaska, Hawaii,
Washington,
Oregon,
California

West North Central
North Dakota,
South Dakota,
Minnesota,
Nebraska, Iowa,
Kansas, Missouri

East North Central
Michigan,
Wisconsin,
Illinois,
Indiana,
Ohio

New England
Maine, New Hampshire,
Vermont, Massachusetts,
Connecticut, Rhode Island

Middle Atlantic
New York,
New Jersey,
Pennsylvania

South Atlantic
Maryland,
Delaware,
West Virginia,
Virginia,
North Carolina,
South Carolina,
Georgia,
Florida

Mountain
Idaho, Montana,
Wyoming, Nevada,
Utah, Colorado,
Arizona, New Mexico

West South Central
Oklahoma, Arkansas,
Texas, Louisiana

East South Central
Kentucky, Tennessee,
Mississippi, Alabama

Here are the same data for the divisions, also ranked from highest to lowest increases.

Division	1-Year	5-Year	Since 1980
Pacific	12.21	62.56	294.99
New England	9.53	67.76	409.01
Middle Atlantic	9.36	51.40	296.28
South Atlantic	8.78	41.19	198.26

West North Central	5.87	36.95	161.26
Mountain	5.46	30.73	170.08
East North Central	4.65	27.37	181.75
East South Central	3.62	20.19	144.16
West South Central	3.22	25.07	88.83

These rankings confirm that the most expensive homes—and the ones that have appreciated the most—are on the East and West Coasts.

OFHEO further breaks down its data into metropolitan statistical areas, or MSAs, which are more useful if you're looking at a specific city or town. Here are the top five MSAs in terms of percentage price increases for the year ended March 31, 2004, along with the five-year totals.

MSA	1-Year	5-Year
Fresno (CA)	21.38	67.28
Riverside–San Bernardino (CA)	20.20	76.34
Fort Pierce–Port St. Lucie (FL)	18.11	65.63
Ventura (CA)	17.77	83.00
Los Angeles–Long Beach (CA)	17.68	72.84

The five MSAs with the lowest rates of appreciation for the last year are:

MSA	1-Year	5-Year
Austin–San Marcos (TX)	0.47	32.95
Boulder–Longmont (CO)	1.34	45.35
Memphis (TN, AR, MS)	1.63	15.13
Montgomery (AL)	1.69	12.84
Provo–Orem (UT)	1.75	10.15

The OFHEO Web site contains information on all of the agency's 220 metropolitan statistical areas as well as other, more detailed, information on home prices around the United States.

COMPARING OTHER COSTS

A specific measure of how widely living costs can vary across the United States was provided in 2004 by Runzheimer International, a management consulting firm based in Rochester, Wisconsin. The firm released partial results of a study on the day-care costs for children that range from more than $1,000 a month in the borough of Manhattan in New York City to less than $340 a month in Baton Rouge, Louisiana. The results were based on full-time day care— five days a week, eight hours a day—for a three-year-old child in a for-profit day-care center. The fourteen most expensive areas for day care, based on monthly costs, were:

Manhattan	$1,057.83
Boston	$977.44
Manchester, New Hampshire	$799.17
Washington, D.C.	$773.36
New London, Connecticut	$748.22
Philadelphia	$740.22
Portland, Oregon	$737.00
Milwaukee, Wisconsin	$673.98
San Francisco	$665.10
Chicago	$657.12
Denver	$654.94
Hartford, Connecticut	$654.33
Detroit	$640.79
Minneapolis	$620.63

The sixteen least expensive areas:

Baton Rouge, Louisiana	$339.44
Mobile, Alabama	$346.67
Winter Haven, Florida	$347.00
Jackson, Mississippi	$362.92
Macon, Georgia	$364.00
Billings, Montana	$373.33
New Orleans, Louisiana	$374.11
Jacksonville, Florida	$375.56
Casper, Wyoming	$376.00
Little Rock, Arkansas	$379.00
Bakersfield, California	$387.78
Miami, Florida	$389.04
Charleston, West Virginia	$400.00
Lafayette, Indiana	$401.56
Columbia, South Carolina	$403.00
Albuquerque, New Mexico	$404.78

A Web site run by the Kaiser Family Foundation—www.kff.org—offers even more proof of some specific differences in costs around the nation, this time for prescription drugs. If you go to the site's, home page, click on "State Health Facts Online" and then on "Health Costs & Budgets," you'll see a link to the average prices of prescriptions around the country. There's even a color-coded map that will allow you to make visual comparisons among the states.

In 2002, the most recent year that data were available, the national average cost of a single prescription was $54.58, up from $49.84 in 2001. However, that same prescription could run from as little as $44.80, or about 18 percent less, in Alabama to $64.81, or 16 percent higher, in Alaska. Here are the rankings of all the states and Washington, D.C.

1.	Alaska	$64.81
2.	New Jersey	$64.76
3.	New York	$63.93
4.	District of Columbia	$63.60
5.	Maryland	$62.22
6.	Minnesota	$61.16
7.	Florida	$58.82
8.	Delaware	$58.25
9.	Connecticut	$58.09
10.	Wisconsin	$57.33
11.	Texas	$56.13
12.	Massachusetts	$55.85
13.	Michigan	$55.15
14.	Missouri	$55.06
15.	Washington	$54.88
16.	Illinois	$54.43
16.	Pennsylvania	$54.43
18.	California	$54.08
19.	Arizona	$53.63
20.	Nebraska	$53.57
21.	Virginia	$53.39
22.	Oklahoma	$53.38
23.	Colorado	$52.79
24.	Idaho	$52.77
25.	Maine	$52.70
26.	Nevada	$52.54
27.	North Carolina	$51.88
28.	New Mexico	$51.63
29.	Kansas	$51.56
30.	Indiana	$51.36
31.	Tennessee	$51.20
32.	Hawaii	$51.18
32.	North Dakota	$51.18
34.	Utah	$51.04

34.	Vermont	$51.04
36.	Rhode Island	$50.84
37.	New Hampshire	$50.51
38.	Ohio	$50.37
39.	Louisiana	$49.95
40.	Montana	$49.60
41.	Georgia	$49.53
42.	South Carolina	$49.50
43.	Iowa	$49.49
44.	Oregon	$49.22
45.	Kentucky	$48.90
46.	Wyoming	$48.55
47.	Mississippi	$48.37
48.	South Dakota	$47.47
49.	West Virginia	$47.31
50.	Arkansas	$45.87
51.	Alabama	$44.80

Day-care and prescription drug expenses, of course, are only a part of any area's cost of living. Local taxes, especially on property, can vary widely, as can the cost of commuting.

4

The Little Things Add Up

It's not about being cheap; it's about being economical.
—STACIA RAGOLIA, EDITOR, *THE FRUGAL WOMAN'S GUIDE TO A RICH LIFE*

Overlooking the little things in your budget as you try to cut expenses can be a big mistake. This is, however, not a call for you to become a tightwad or deny yourself things you need or want. It is about living well, being a smart spender, and maximizing the power of your money. When you cut spending, you increase income.

The trick to saving money on little things is to be sure you actually save the money and don't fritter it away on some other little thing. Suppose, for instance, you buy two cans of soda a day at work from a machine. Typically, they cost about $1 each. That's $2 a day: $10 a week and $40 a month. If you buy a case of your favorite soda at a discount store, it usually ends up costing less than 25 cents a can. So if you bring your two cans of soda to work each day, you save $1.50: $7.50 a week and $30 a month. Save that $30 each month for twenty years at 6 percent interest and you'll have $13,861.22; in thirty years, you'll have $30,135.45. You will have deprived yourself of nothing; you will still have had your two sodas each day. But this only works if you set $1.50 aside each day and at the end of the month stick the $30 into your savings account or mutual fund. Avoid the temptation to look on the $1.50 as loose change that gets spent on something else.

Do you spend $10 a day for lunch at a restaurant or a deli? Take your lunch for about $2 a day and pocket the $8 difference. That's $160 a month. In twenty years at 6 percent, you'll have $73,926.54; in thirty years, $160,722.40. Again, you will have given up nothing. In fact, you might have gained in the health department because your own food will probably be better for you than what you would have bought.

Later in this chapter, we'll look at some more examples of savings on little things and how they can add up to big bucks.

A RICH LIFE

Stacia Ragolia is the vice president of community and services at iVillage, which operates the www.iVillage.com Web site on financial and other issues specifically for women. She is also the editor of *The Frugal Woman's Guide to a Rich Life* (Rutledge Hill Press, 2003). The book is a compilation of advice from visitors to www.iVillage.com about simplifying life and saving money. Although women are its target readers, its advice appeals to men and women alike.

Ragolia said in an interview that her book reflected more than just cutting expenses. When you reject mindless consumerism, you not only save money but also reap psychological rewards. She pointed, for example, to pricey commercial cleaning supplies that are often designed to clean only certain things so that you are forced to buy several different products for various household cleaning jobs. "The consumer packaged good industry tries to get us to spend money on a product that does just one little thing," she said. "White vinegar mixed with water cleans just about everything as well as or better than those commercial cleaners—and at a fraction of the price. This mix is also better for the environment, compared with a lot of those commercial cleaning supplies. So it makes you more conscious of how your spending habits can affect the environment, while you're introducing fewer toxins into your house. The focus here is on what is a rich life. It's one in which you feel safe and comfortable, one in which you don't have to worry that some chemical you used to clean a rug will harm your children. And what you have used cleans just as well and costs a lot less."

Ragolia emphasized that she does not advocate depriving yourself or living cheaply. Like Walker Smith, she believes that there is no link between money and happiness. "We all like having nice things," she said, "but there are plenty of ways to have nice things without spending too much money. It's not about being cheap; it's about being economical. It's about creating in-depth, meaningful life experiences that move your money around in ways that benefit you more—whether you're investing it or using it for some other goal. Getting more enjoyment out of life does not mean throwing money at things. It's not just about the money you save. You can actually have a better life simplifying and changing your spending habits. A lot of this is about being happy."

She cited five areas where people can easily cut expenses and avoid debts—and still live well:

- Groceries and related items
- Clothing
- Home furnishings and decorating
- Family activities
- Holiday spending

In addition to making your own cleaning solution with vinegar and water, you can buy items on sale and use coupons to save money at the grocery store. (Ragolia noted that coupon use rises with shoppers' education levels.) "Especially pay attention to double and triple coupon days at your supermarket," she said. "It can really make a difference in your grocery bill, and it's very important to get a handle on weekly grocery spending."

She also recommended joining food co-ops to buy directly from wholesalers; if there are no co-ops in your town, consider organizing one made up of like-minded people in your neighborhood who can rotate buying and distribution duties. Co-ops can be especially useful for obtaining organic food, which is usually more expensive because it's harder to distribute and there are few outlets. If co-ops don't appeal to you, Ragolia said, you can share bulk purchases from buying clubs like Costco or Sam's Club with neighbors and friends: "This is in some ways simpler than getting involved in a very organized co-op program where you're buying a lot of stuff." She added that you should take a hard look at what you need when making bulk purchases so as not to overbuy. "It's also important," she continued, "that when you're shopping at a place like Costco you differentiate between a want and a need."

This advice on grocery shopping may sound elementary. Food and related expenses, however, can be a big source of excessive and impulse spending. Poor planning is often at fault. Most of the time when my wife and I order a twenty-dollar pizza delivered to our house or go to a mediocre neighborhood restaurant and drop thirty dollars on dinner, it's because we have neglected shopping and have nothing at home that is appealing for dinner, or we're tired and don't feel like preparing food. A little planning—keeping enough food in the house and storing some prepared easy-to-fix meals in the freezer—could help eliminate this kind of impulse spending. It might also increase happiness, since my wife and I are rarely satisfied—either with the food or with the financial outlay—after one of these spur-of-the-moment meals. It's a better value for your money to dine out when you're doing so for its own sake at a place you really like rather than as a panic reaction to being tired or out of groceries.

Ragolia said one of the secrets of buying clothes is to break our old consumer habits of being concerned about what's hot for the season. Instead, stick for the most part to brand-name classic clothes that do not go out of style. "In retail, there is usually a short full-price period and then a sales period," she noted. "At the Gap, for instance, most merchandise gets discounted four to six weeks after it comes out. So you can save a good deal just by waiting a bit." In addition to shopping at outlets, you can save money via e-mail and the Internet. "There are lots of good e-mail-based savings," Ragolia reported. "This is one time when being on a mailing list is good. L.L. Bean, for example, sends out e-mail alerts when things go on sale. I just picked up a pair of shoes for my son for five dollars. They're a good, solid pair of L.L. Bean moccasins that are well made and won't fall apart, that will last him for a long time. It's often worth buying brand-name merchandise because it usually lasts longer. Learn to figure out what stuff lasts longer. If you have to choose between spending fifty dollars for a pair of shoes that will last four years and twenty dollars on a pair you will have to replace in six months, there is obviously a long-term savings in buying the more expensive pair."

One thing I learned from living for several years in Europe, where clothes are more expensive than in the United States, is to seek out stores that sell high-end used clothing. Some of these garments have never been worn or have been worn only once or twice. These stores are excellent sources for tuxedos and evening wear that you will only use occasionally. You can often save hundreds of dollars on top-quality clothes, and no one will ever know the difference.

Ragolia's comment about classic styles reminded me of the time, twenty years ago, when I had admired a blue blazer in the window of a fancy store on Madison Avenue in New York. But its price tag was $400—far too expensive for my budget. Several months later, I saw a big sale sign on the store's window and went in. There was the blazer I had admired, in my size, on sale for half price. It was next to a rack of new blazers that looked identical. I asked a sales clerk why the blazer I had admired was on sale. "It's the buttons," he sniffed. "They're silver. Everyone wants gold this year." I bought the silver-buttoned blazer knowing that I could survive the humiliation if I found myself in a room full of people wearing gold-buttoned blazers. Had I invested the $200 I saved on that blazer at 6 percent interest, it would have grown to $662.04 by now. Of course, this was a discretionary item and I spent as much as I could afford for it. The $200 I saved I really didn't have to put aside; it wasn't a true savings because I would never spend more than $200 on a blazer. That's the same reason I didn't put $285 in the bank when I recently bought a pair of $385 Mephisto shoes for $100 on eBay. I wouldn't have paid more than $100 for a pair of shoes anyway. At least that's my excuse, and I'm sticking to it.

Home furnishings and decorating are another area where you can realize great savings. As Ragolia put it, they present an opportunity to "take advantage of other people's bad spending habits. . . . There are plenty of people who want to change their dining room every three years." Charity thrift shops and eBay can be good sources for high-quality furniture at substantial savings. If a dining room set at a retail furniture store is $2,000, it's very likely that with a little searching you can find a good used one of equal or better quality for $500. That $1,500 you save will turn into almost $5,000 in twenty years at 6 percent. And you'll probably still be enjoying the $500 dining room set. Ragolia also cited the example of custom-colored paint. Such paint can cost as much as fifty dollars a gallon, but you don't have to pay full price if you are somewhat flexible about the colors you want. That's because paint stores often have cans of custom paint that have been returned that sell for as little as five dollars a gallon. She also recommended using maps on one wall of a room instead of high-priced wallpaper. (Another tip: use fluorescent lightbulbs and make sure your home is well insulated; both will save on energy costs.)

"All these little things really add up," Ragolia said. "You can buy stuff you can be happy with for a long time without wrecking your budget. Yard sales and thrift shops, if you take them as an adventure, can not only be good for your budget; they can be fun. They also are usually cash-based, which can help you avoid credit card debt. In fact, shopping with cash—taking only what you can afford to spend and no more—can be key to keeping to your budget. Leave the credit cards at home. If you don't have the credit card, you won't make the impulse purchase."

Another area ripe for savings that Ragolia cited is family activities, especially those involving children. How many times have you seen dads at the concession stand in a movie theater spending thirty dollars on outrageously overpriced soda, popcorn, hot dogs, and the like? This on top of the thirty to forty dollars it can often cost a family of four just to buy movie tickets. "Try to focus on activities that don't involve spending a lot of money," she said. "Games, for instance, or a family night when you talk to each other. That's actually a revolutionary idea for America! The point is, you can have a good time without spending forty dollars to sit in a dark room and not interact with your family. And you don't have to deny yourself anything. If you really want to see a movie, rent it for a fraction of the price of taking four or more people to a movie theater. These, again, are fairly small things. But if you've been spending forty dollars a week on movies, that's more than two thousand dollars a year. With this savings, you would have enough at the end of the year for a nice family vacation."

The fifth area Ragolia cited is holiday spending. It is a source of debt for many people who get caught up in the four- to six-week shopping frenzy leading up to Christmas. A better strategy is to buy gifts, especially when they are on sale, throughout the year. "Buying things when they're on sale can really help," she said. "For example, if someone you normally give a gift to is a gardener, buy him or her some garden equipment when it goes on sale in mid-summer." She also recommended being imaginative about gifts. "We all have so much; most of us don't really need anything. Why not give your time, or make things for people. Baby-sitting for a friend could be your gift. Or cooking a meal or a special dish. Remember, this is about having a rich life and being happy. I hate to go to the mall in December. If you've done your shopping throughout the year, when mid-November rolls around you can actually have time to enjoy your family during the holidays instead of running around shopping."

Ragolia said that people often think too big when it comes to savings: "They think they can't save any money unless they save ten thousand dollars at a time. But one or two hundred dollars a week saved from cutting the things we've mentioned can easily grow to ten thousand dollars in a year or so." She strongly suggested that some of the money saved from the five areas she discussed go into an emergency fund. "When you have some money saved up, you can avoid going into debt for an emergency. That's the way a lot of people end up in debt and in trouble. They have a health emergency or a house problem; if they have no financial buffer, suddenly they're in debt."

Ragolia's comments only scratch the surface of the advice in her book and in a number of other books on how to save money. There are also plenty of Web sites that can be of assistance. At www.iVillage.com, for example, you can sign up for a "Free Stuff" newsletter, and www.practicalmoneyskills.com offers basic help with personal finances. The Web sites run by personal-finance magazines like *Smart Money* (www.smartmoney.com), *Kiplinger's* (www.kiplinger.com), and *Money* (www.money.com) can also be helpful. In addition, there are numerous online calculators to help you with various financial and savings calculations and projections. Some of my favorites are at www.mortgages.interest.com. At the bottom of the home page, click on the calculators listed.

THE POWER OF COMPOUND SAVINGS

Let's apply some of these savings ideas to a hypothetical couple with two children, ages nine and eleven. We'll assume that they live in a typical three-bedroom suburban home, that both parents work, and that the family goes to the movies three nights a month. Now let's see what they can conservatively save without giving up anything, and what the savings will mean one year, two years, five years, ten years, and twenty years from now.

The parents each spend an average of $10 a day on lunch. They decide to take a $2 lunch from home on Tuesdays and Thursdays, saving $32 a week, or $128 a month. Both agree to stop buying a $1 can of soda each day from machines at work and instead buy the same soda by the case at a discount store and carry the drinks to work at a cost of 25 cents a can. That saves $1.50 a day, or $30 a month.

They start paying close attention to their grocery bills, using coupons where possible, and join a Costco buying club. They conservatively estimate they can cut their grocery bills by $30 a week, or $120 a month.

They have been spending about $40 three times a month going

Figure 6

Small Economies Add Up

Skipping a few dollars' worth of minor expenses each month can add substantially to savings over the long haul. These examples are based on a 6 percent return on savings.

	Monthly savings	Cumulative savings				
		1 year	2 years	5 years	10 years	20 years
Lunch	$128	$1,578.95	$3,255.29	$ 8,930.56	$20,976.55	$ 59,141.23
Sodas	30	370.06	762.95	2,093.10	4,916.38	13,861.22
Groceries	120	1,480.20	3,051.83	8,372.40	19,665.52	55,444.90
Movies	72	888.16	1,831.10	5,023.44	11,799.31	33,266.94
Total	$350	**$4,317.37**	**$8,901.17**	**$24,419.50**	**$57,357.76**	**$161,714.29**

to the movies, including overpriced goodies from the concession stand. They decide to cut their movie trips to once a month and rent two movies a month for about $4 each. That saves $72 a month.

This family can certainly make further savings on clothing, home furnishings, and holiday spending, but let's look just at these initial, easy savings of $350 a month that have required them to sacrifice nothing. We will assume, of course, that each month they put aside the money they have saved and that it earns an average of 6 percent interest.

As figure 6 illustrates, in twenty years the family will have saved $161,714.29. Compound interest and time can turn little things into big savings. After only a year the family has saved more than $4,000, which could be important as a buffer in case of an emergency. As Ragolio pointed out, it could keep them from going into debt for unexpected spending.

5

Insurance: What You Need, What You Don't

*You are three times more likely to become disabled
than to die during your working years.*

—DEENA KATZ, FINANCIAL ADVISER AND PLANNER

Insurance is complicated and confusing. Many people have more than they need or less than they need or have the wrong kind or pay too much for it. Others have it for the wrong reasons.

If you think of insurance in terms of "risk management," it may be easier to tackle your choices. We all have risks in our lives; some are insurable, and some are not. The risk that your house may burn to the ground is an insurable event. You can't really save to replace the house, because if it catches fire next week, you would not have enough time to save the money you need. Instead you insure against the possible loss by paying into a fund that will reimburse you if the event occurs.

Deena Katz, the financial adviser introduced in chapter 2, divides insurance into two categories: that which is a "given," meaning you should never be without it, and insurance that may be necessary, but not always, depending on your circumstances and needs. You cannot afford to be without health insurance and property and casualty insurance (automobile and homeowners' coverage). "Without these, you can instantly go broke," she stated. "They are not options." She ranks other insurance in order of descending importance: disability, life, and long-term care. (Later in this chapter we'll take a detailed look at health insurance, which many people don't have—or can't afford—despite Katz's no-option warning.)

Consumers have little control over property and casualty insurance because it is for the most part mandated by states, mortgage lenders, or automobile finance companies, although its costs can vary widely from state to state. (Chapter 7 discusses automobile costs, including insurance.) Moving to a less expensive area can make a big difference in the amount of money you spend for insurance. Otherwise, to cut expenses on coverage you are often limited to increasing your deductible amounts and eliminating frills. Some companies may be cheaper than others, but they may not be as reliable for speedy payments on and resolutions of claims. They also may be quicker to cancel your coverage if you have multiple claims. Keep in mind that not all companies sell property and casualty insurance in all states. *Consumer Reports* magazine remains one of the best sources of information on this type of insurance.

The purpose of this chapter is not to delve into the ever-changing details and prices of various kinds of insurance policies but rather to present an overview that will hopefully help you better understand your needs. This, in turn, will show you how to generate savings—especially with the insurance that is less important. The section on health insurance, however, because of its importance, does contain some specifics on prices to allow meaningful comparisons; it is the longest part of the chapter for good reason: poll after poll shows that health care and paying for it are among Americans' top concerns.

THE OTHER INSURANCE

Katz recommends viewing insurance as the solution to a potential problem: if you don't have the potential problem, or the chances of it are miniscule, you don't need the insurance.

Katz also suggests that you consult a financial adviser—preferably an independent one who charges a fee for services and doesn't sell any financial products like mutual funds or annuities—in addition to an insurance agent. "Many times insurance agents come up with insurance as the answer to all problems, including your investment problems," she said. "Don't confuse insurance with investing." Be wary, for example, of life insurance agents who promote their policies as investments.

The National Association of Personal Financial Advisors has a Web site (www.napfa.org) that can help you find a financial adviser in your area, and the Certified Financial Planner Board of Standards (www.cpfboard.org), can tell you if an adviser has been the source of any consumer complaints. Try to find an adviser whose typical client's assets match yours. According to the *Wall Street Journal,* you can expect to pay between $100 and $400 an hour for a financial adviser, or a flat fee usually starting at $1,000 for a set number of meetings. Those fees may seem high, but if the advice offered saves only a few hundred dollars a year, over ten, twenty, or thirty years the savings will far exceed the fees.

Disability Insurance

Katz ranks disability insurance as the most important of other insurance. "You are three times more likely to become disabled than to die during your working years," she said. "Being able to earn income is probably your biggest asset. You need to protect that."

Good disability policies, however, are expensive and increasingly difficult to get. Many workers receive this insurance as a benefit through their jobs, but Katz believes these work-related policies often aren't very good because of how they define *disability*, or they offer only short-term instead of long-term coverage, leaving you with income gaps when you most need assistance. "What you want is a policy that will pay if you can't work in your 'own occupation,'" she explained. "Many policies say you must not be able to work in 'any occupation' before they will pay. That's a higher threshold. What you want is income replacement, cash if you can't work at your regular job. If you can get these policies through your work, that's the first place to look. But you may have to consider a supplemental private policy."

An interesting wrinkle in the income tax laws is that whether you pay taxes on income-replacement payments from disability insurance depends on who paid the premiums. If you did, the money is tax-free; if your employer paid, you'll owe taxes. For most people, however, the decision about who pays for disability insurance as part of a benefits package is made by their employer. Of course, the income-replacement payments from any private policy you pay for yourself would be tax-free.

Life Insurance

Do you need life insurance?

Katz says the two major functions of life insurance are to replace income and to preserve an estate after taxes, say in the case of a family-owned business. "If you don't have any children or estate-planning issues or don't have to replace your income, what do you need life insurance for?" she asks. Some people, of course, carry life insurance to *create* an estate for their children. If their children are not dependents, however, is the life insurance necessary? What income is it replacing? What problem is it solving? Katz argues that most people, as they get older and their assets build, have less and less need for life insurance.

Here are some insurance terms you should understand:

- *Whole life* is insurance that is linked to a fixed-rate investment so that it builds cash value, which is fixed—along with the death benefit and premium—when the policy is issued. Whole life is the most expensive kind of coverage. It can cost thousands of dollars a year, compared with a same-value term policy costing hundreds of dollars a year.

- *Universal life* combines term life insurance with a marketlike return. The cash buildup is not fixed or guaranteed and can be used to pay the premiums when you get older. This, of course, would lower the death benefit. Also, if interest rates drop, you may have to increase your premiums to maintain coverage.
- *Variable life* invests some of your premiums into stock and bond mutual funds. Cash value is not guaranteed, and the death benefits depend on how well the investments have performed.
- *Term insurance* pays a set amount if you die while the policy is in force and never accrues any cash value. The policy is written for a set term, say ten or twenty years. *Level-premium term* charges the same amount for each year of coverage. When the term ends, that's it; if you want more insurance, you have to qualify for it and start over again. *Annual renewable term* lets you purchase it year by year at increasingly higher premiums. You can renew your coverage annually without proof of good health, but at some point you will probably balk at the premiums.

If you do need life insurance, Katz recommends term insurance in most cases. "Pay for what you need, for the time that you need it. Say until your kids get out of school. Term insurance is cheap; just be sure it's guaranteed for the period needed and they can't change the rates. An exception I would allow to term insurance might be, say, if you have a disabled child; then you may need some insurance that builds value like whole life or universal, or variable life if you're young."

Katz warns against buying life insurance for children in most cases. "Children don't have incomes. What is the problem you're trying to solve? Invest some money for them instead. My mother bought life insurance for me when I was three months old. When I was eighteen, I got a two-hundred-dollar check from the insurance company. What if she had instead put money in a mutual fund for eighteen years?" That check could have been for thousands instead of hundreds.

Long-Term-Care Insurance

There are no easy answers regarding long-term-care insurance. It is getting more expensive and covering less; worse still, the regulations governing it are inconsistent. Existing policyholders can also face premium increases, especially for policies that were underpriced in recent years as insurers tried to gain market share. The AARP Web site (www.aarp.org) cites the case of an Ohio couple who saw the annual premiums on their eight-year-old policy jump from $3,255 to $4,862, a 50 percent increase. According to the May 2004 issue of *Kiplinger's Retirement Report,* twenty-one states have adopted model regulations drafted by the National Association of Insurance Commissioners (NAIC) to stabilize premiums; policies purchased prior to passage of the regulations in each state, however, are not covered, *Kiplinger's* points out.

The regulations and other state-by-state reforms have made a difference, and there is relatively better standardization of these policies than in the past. This is especially important, Katz says, when it comes to the definitions of events that will trigger benefit payments. Keep in mind, too, that long-term care doesn't only mean moving to a nursing home. Many policies will also pay for home care if you need it. The NAIC Web site (www.naic.org) contains information on the group's regulatory proposals for long-term care, as well as links to the various state insurance departments. Some of these links are helpful, some less so. In the end, you may have to contact your state insurance department for its regulations, or proposed regulations, on long-term-care insurance. Some states offer tax incentives for buying this type of insurance. Don't forget to check with your company's benefits department. Long-term-care insurance is sometimes offered through employers at more favorable rates.

"Long-term-care insurance is hard to understand, it varies with every state, and it is not the panacea we would like it to be," Katz said. "On the other hand, there are good uses for it. And needing long-term care sure is an insurable event. The reasons people should buy long-term care are for asset protection, estate preservation, and what I call the fear factor: if someone lives far away from their family and there is no one to take care of them, it is certainly a lot easier to go into a long-term-care facility as a paying patient than to have to go broke and accept Medicaid. The insurance is expensive, but you may be willing to accept a lesser quality of life today—in other words, bear the cost of buying the insurance—for the promise of tomorrow. The younger you are when you buy it, of course, the less the premiums are."

Most experts agree that the two groups of people who should not purchase long-term-care insurance are those who have enough money to afford care on their own and those with too few assets to worry about protecting. The latter group would just count on Medicaid taking over after they have exhausted their resources. The only problem is that in many states this can adversely affect the assets of the spouse who doesn't need long-term care. Advice on this topic is available from county and state agencies for the aging.

The question, of course, is how high and low your assets must be. Katz uses $200,000 as the asset level—including equity in your home—below which you probably can't afford long-term-care insurance. "There are disagreements about this all the time," she said. "Some advisers say one hundred thousand dollars. It depends on whether you're married." Those with high levels of assets just have to make a decision about what they can afford. "The average nursing home stay runs about thirty-five hundred dollars a month," she reported. "The average stay is about ninety days. Those that stay longer than that stay about three years. But at the tail end of those statistics are people who are in nursing homes for many years."

What about those whose assets fall in the middle range? If you are single, aren't concerned about leaving an estate, or do not live away from people who can help you, you may not need long-term-care insurance. Katz advises taking your family medical background into consideration. "Does your family history include Alzheimer's disease or rheumatoid arthritis—things that would incapacitate you for a long period of time? If you're in that gene pool, you may want to consider long-term-care insurance more than the guy next door who doesn't have these illnesses in his family background."

Forget About It

The July 2004 issue of *Consumer Reports* magazine published a list of ten kinds of insurance you probably don't need. These policies cover events that often fall under health, property and casualty, disability, and life insurance policies.

- Credit-card-loss protection. You're already protected under federal law for anything more than fifty dollars per card.
- Identity-theft insurance. This covers the costs of repairing your credit, but not for unauthorized charges or funds taken from accounts. Keep a close eye on your credit report instead.
- Car-rental insurance. You're probably already covered by your credit card or your own auto policy.
- Flight insurance. Your health plan and life insurance provide coverage.
- Cancer insurance. The odds are you're already covered through your health plan.
- Mortgage life insurance. It's more expensive than term life insurance, and its benefits decline as you pay your mortgage down.
- Accidental-death insurance. Death is death, and only about 5 percent of those who die each year do so in an accident. Regular term life insurance pays regardless of the cause of death.

- Credit-life insurance will pay off credit card debt or other loans if you die. So will term life insurance, which is much less expensive.
- Credit disability insurance will make your loan payments if you are disabled—as will a regular disability plan. It does not, however, replace income for other expenses.
- Involuntary unemployment insurance takes care of your loan payments if you are laid off. *Consumer Reports* recommends creating an emergency fund instead that will cover three to six months of your expenses.

HEALTH INSURANCE: THE 800-POUND GORILLA

While health insurance is the most important kind of insurance for us to have, there are a shocking number of people in America who live without it. Even those who have it, whether through their jobs or private policies, are under increasing financial pressure as benefits are going down while premiums are going up. Most people are only a layoff or a downsizing away from joining the ranks of the uninsured. If you have company-paid health insurance, it's a good idea to know what your options are if you should lose it. If you're already paying for private insurance, there may be some less expensive alternatives you should be aware of.

A 2004 study by Families USA, a nonprofit consumer health organization based in Washington, D.C., found that 81.8 million people—a third of the population under sixty-five years old—lacked health insurance at some point in 2003 and 2004, and most of those were uninsured for more than nine months. People sixty-five and older, of course, are covered by Medicare.

The Census Bureau puts the number of uninsured at 43.6 million but counts only those who were uninsured for all of 2002.

The Families USA study, based mainly on census data, showed that almost two-thirds of those lacking insurance (65.3 percent) were uninsured for six months or more; slightly more than half (50.6

percent) were uninsured for at least nine months. The states where more than a third of nonelderly people had no insurance were:

	Percentage
Texas	43.4
New Mexico	42.4
California	37.1
Nevada	36.8
Louisiana	36.2
Arizona	35.7
Mississippi	35.1
Alaska	35.0
Oklahoma	35.0
Florida	34.6
Arkansas	34.4
Idaho	33.8
North Carolina	33.7
New York	33.4

This is not a just a problem of the poor or unemployed. Four out of five of the uninsured were in working families, according to the study. Of those working families, significant portions of the middle class were found to be uninsured. For example, among people with annual incomes between 300 and 400 percent of the federal poverty level (between $55,980 and $74,640 for a family of four in 2003), more than one out of four were uninsured. Even among families with incomes of $75,000 and up, 13.5 million people were without insurance for part of 2002 and 2003.

While there is much talk about uninsured children, this is a problem for Americans throughout their prime working years. Here is the breakdown of the uninsured by age:

Age	Percentage
0 to 17	36.7
18 to 24	50.3
25 to 44	32.9
45 to 54	20.7
55 to 64	17.3

"The growing number of Americans without health insurance is now a phenomenon that significantly affects middle-class and working families," said Ron Pollack, the executive director of Families USA, in a statement accompanying the study. "As a result, this problem is no longer simply an altruistic issue affecting the poor, but a matter of self-interest for almost everyone."

That's putting it mildly. In fact, the United States is one of the few modern nations that doesn't offer some form of national health insurance to all its citizens, regardless of where they work or whether they work at all. Our health-care system is in shambles and is not likely to get better soon. Congress, under the sway of drug companies and big for-profit health-care corporations, lurches from one piecemeal solution to the next without coming close to a comprehensive solution. Yet despite—or, more likely, because of—the number of uninsured, the United States spends more per capita on health care than other industrialized countries and gets less. A 2000 study by Dr. Barbara Starfield of the Johns Hopkins School of Medicine found that of thirteen countries, the United States ranked an average of twelfth for sixteen health indicators: thirteenth—dead last—in low-birth-weight percentages; thirteenth for neonatal mortality and infant mortality overall; thirteenth for years of life lost, excluding external causes; eleventh for life expectancy at the age of one for females and twelfth for males; and tenth for life expectancy at the age of fifteen for females and twelfth for males. At the time of the study, Japan ranked highest among developed countries in terms of health. In an interview in

2004, Dr. Starfield told Bob Herbert of the *New York Times* that the situation was getting worse. She called the data "incontrovertible."

Our large population of uninsured is a big contributor to both America's high health-care costs and poor rankings. That's because people without insurance often don't get much preventive care and usually don't seek treatment until problems are more advanced— and thus more difficult and expensive to treat. When the uninsured do seek treatment, it's usually through expensive hospital emergency rooms rather than a lower-cost visit to a doctor's office.

There have been moves over the years to bring universal health coverage to America, but all have met with failure. The most recent major effort was former president Bill Clinton's proposal in the early 1990s. There have also been failed efforts to extend Medicare to everyone.

One of the most interesting proposals for a type of universal coverage was made in 1972 by the late senator Russell B. Long, a Louisiana Democrat. It was called federal catastrophic health insurance and enjoyed a degree of bipartisan support, although Congress never passed it. It was ahead of its time and may still be. Senator Long's plan would have had the government pay all medical costs above an annual deductible of $2,000 for those not covered by Medicare. (Today, of course, that deductible might be more like $8,000 to $10,000.) Insurance companies would have underwritten much of the government's coverage. In addition, they could have sold private policies covering the deductible portion. For people who couldn't afford the deductible or insurance for it, Medicaid would have paid.

It's difficult to find fault with this plan. It would have included participation by private insurance companies and would have covered everyone. People who did not qualify for Medicaid could have paid the deductible themselves, bought insurance for it, or had coverage provided by their employers. Because insurance companies' exposure for the deductible would have been limited to paying a relatively small, capped amount each year, such policies would have been much less expensive than conventional ones. Because costs would be low, it would have taken much of the health-care burden off companies, and small businesses would have been encouraged to offer deductible coverage to their workers.

Federal catastrophic health insurance would for the most part avoid the bureaucracy that many people fear with national health insurance, since most Americans would be unlikely to ever use it. For people over sixty-five, who usually have the biggest medical expenses, coverage would be provided by Medicare.

Jay Constantine, who worked for the Senate Finance Committee in the 1970s when Senator Long was chairman, believes there was nothing wrong with the plan—then or now. "It empowers people," he said. "It gives them health care separate from corporations or their employers. This is especially important in the kind of mobile society we have now. It is the right track and the least costly approach to getting everybody covered." Interestingly, as we shall see later in this chapter, Senator Long's concept did not die entirely; a faint echo of it—without universal coverage or direct government financial backup—has returned in the form of health savings accounts.

The End of an Era

Over the years, most people have been provided with health insurance through their jobs and given little thought to health-care costs. That era is rapidly coming to an end as companies, faced with rising costs, have shifted more costs to workers or cut back on coverage. This has usually taken the form of increased premium-sharing by workers, increased copayments for prescription drugs and medical services, and higher annual deductibles. These increases have taken a big bite out of our disposable incomes. There's not much an individual can do, however, because insurance through your job is still the cheapest way to go.

The bigger problem is for those people who have no coverage

through their jobs and must purchase private insurance. There are two problems with private insurance: it is expensive, and it can exclude preexisting conditions. In all but a few states, it can be extremely difficult—often impossible—to get coverage for a preexisting condition.

Your access to an individual policy depends to a large degree on where you live. The states have varying laws that govern access to health insurance. Two terms you need to become familiar with are *guaranteed-issue laws* and *community rating*. According to data from eHealthInsurance, a big online broker that is the largest source of health insurance for individuals and small businesses in the United States, there are five states with guaranteed-issue laws: Maine, Massachusetts, New Jersey, New York, and Vermont. Their laws vary, but the bottom line is that any insurance company offering individual policies in these states has to sell you insurance regardless of your preexisting conditions, although there can be a waiting period. Usually, insurers in guaranteed-issue states can't cancel your policy unless they pull out of the market in your state. Because insurers in these states have to take all comers, regardless of preexisting health conditions, the policies are comparatively expensive. But at least you can get them.

If you are healthy and have no preexisting medical conditions, buying private insurance should not be difficult in a state without guaranteed-issue laws. Remember, however, that a health insurance policy that doesn't cover preexisting conditions can be an invitation to trouble. Even if you get a policy that covers everything, you could face big premium increases if you get sick—again, depending on the state in which you live.

Which brings us to *community rating*. Most states allow insurers to base premiums for individual policies on a client's age and health. The exceptions are the same five states with guaranteed-issue laws—Maine, Massachusetts, New Jersey, New York, and Vermont—which also have community rating. This means insurers have to charge everyone who lives in the state the same premium for a particular policy regardless of age or health. Premiums can be raised only for all policyholders; individuals or groups of individuals cannot be singled out for increases. Since these states also have guaranteed-issue laws, there is little competition among insurance companies and premiums are high. But again, you can at least get the insurance and can't be singled out for a rate increase.

State laws change all the time. A good source for current information on health insurance in various states is the Web site (www.health insuranceinfo.net) run by Georgetown University's Health Policy Institute.

States without guaranteed-issue laws or community rating have the lowest premiums, but you may not be able to get the insurance because insurers are allowed to "cherry pick" the healthiest clients. If you can't get insurance in one of those states, you could be forced into high-risk insurance pools with very steep rates and sometimes long waiting lists.

A good place to check out prices for individual policies is eHealthInsurance's Web site (www.ehealthinsurance.com). You don't have to register, and you can browse prices anonymously. All you need to provide is a zip code and a date of birth, and indicate whether you are a smoker or a student. If you want to apply for insurance, you can do so online; there is also a toll-free number (800-977-8860) for help and additional information. We'll look at some premiums later, but clearly the best scenario for buying an individual policy is that your health is good and you live in, or will move to, one of the states with no guaranteed-issue laws or community rating. This will give you the best deal initially. But remember, insurers in these states may be able to raise your rates—sometimes by a lot—if you come down with a serious illness. If you have health issues, you're probably better off in a state like New York or New Jersey, where insurance and rates are guaranteed, even though the cost of insurance is higher.

If you don't have health insurance because you have been laid off or left your job for any reason other than gross misconduct, you can extend your company's coverage for eighteen months under a federal law known as COBRA. When COBRA benefits expire, you can get insurance under another federal law called HIPAA. These laws are often used by early retirees who are not yet sixty-five and thus ineligible for Medicare, but anyone can take advantage of them. The rules are further explained in chapter 9, which looks at some of the retirement issues that may come up in your financial planning.

Congress to the Rescue—for Some

Health savings accounts, or HSAs, are the latest wrinkle in health-care policies. These accounts are aimed at helping those who must buy their own insurance, but they are also designed to help companies lower the costs of providing worker health coverage. HSAs were created in late 2003 when Congress approved the limited prescription drug benefit for Medicare beneficiaries that is set to take effect in 2006. Although HSAs don't solve the big problems we have discussed, they do have the potential to make private health policies less expensive—and therefore accessible—for more people.

HSAs must be established in conjunction with a catastrophic health insurance policy that, because of its high deductible, is cheaper. Money you put in an HSA each year can be deducted from your income tax and used to pay the deductible portion of your health-care expenses. The account is somewhat like an individual retirement account. If you use the money you contribute to the plan, or any of the investment income that money earns, for anything but medical expenses, you must pay taxes and a 10 percent penalty on the amount withdrawn. The account balance can build year to year. When you are sixty-five and eligible for Medicare, you can use the HSA funds for anything you want; if, at that point, you spend the money on nonmedical expenses, however, you must pay taxes on it (but no penalty).

For individuals, insurance plans must have a deductible of $1,000 or more to be eligible for a companion HSA; for families, the deductible must be $2,000 or more. Individuals can make a contribution to an HSA in any amount up to the insurance plan's deductible but not more than $2,600 per year; families can put in up to $5,150 per year. Both of these limits are inflation-indexed and will increase. If your insurance policy has a higher deductible than the annual limit, the difference is your responsibility. The yearly indexed out-of-pocket maximum, however, is $5,000 for an individual and $10,000 for a family, regardless of your catastrophic plan. Remember, too, that an HSA's value can build year to year.

"Ideally, the deductible on your policy would match the maximum on your HSA. But yes, there could be a gap if you picked a higher deductible policy," said Robert Hurley, the chief operating officer of Health Savings Account Solutions for eHealthInsurance. "But since the account builds year to year, that gap will disappear. I recommend buying a policy with a deductible that matches your HSA, then increase the deductible—and lower your premiums—as your savings build."

As of this writing, HSAs are available in thirty-one states, and most experts expect they will eventually be available in all states. The holdup is that some state laws and regulations must be tweaked or revoked to allow HSA-eligible policies. "The pressure on the market to provide these plans is building," Hurley noted. "It's going to take more time in these states where the regulations and laws need to be changed, but consumers are going to demand it."

The reason for the ballooning consumer demand: a great price. In some states, an individual can get an HSA-eligible high-deductible policy for as little as $100 a month—sometimes less.

There are two main criticisms of HSAs. One is that they are of no help to working families who aren't eligible for Medicaid but can't afford to fund an HSA, much less pay insurance premiums. The other is that people may neglect routine preventive care if they have to spend their own money for it before they reach their deductible. "The problem of those who truly can't afford any insurance is a whole other issue," Hurley said. "We need to subsidize them in some way; the government will have to have some role in providing coverage to those folks. But if you look at the total number of uninsured, around half could actually afford health insurance but don't buy it. Why? I believe the reason is that they think the premiums are so high they are flushing money down a black hole." Hurley thinks that lower premiums might lure some of the uninsured into the insurance market. He also cited two studies of the health-care industry that indicated that people may become more attentive to preventive care if they believe paying for it will save them money in the long run. He pointed out that HSA money can be used to pay for treatments that are not always covered by a regular insurance policy, like programs to lose weight or stop smoking.

"What we're seeing is that these HSAs are bringing the individual consumer back into the health-insurance equation," Hurley said. "One of the biggest challenges for businesses is the lack of predictability in health-care costs. It's possible we can create a system with HSAs in which employers will have a more predictable contribution to employee health care." Hurley's comment about the individual consumer points to one of the real pluses of HSAs: they give you more control over your health care and what gets covered.

On the other hand, HSAs won't help if you are one of those individuals with preexisting conditions who is only able to get insurance—expensive insurance—in states with guaranteed-issue laws. One problem with guaranteed-issue laws is that people *can* wait until they are sick to buy insurance. "It's like buying homeowner's insurance when your house is on fire," Hurley said. Being able to buy insurance when you're sick, of course, means higher premiums, which put the insurance out of reach for more people. Guaranteed-issue doesn't means guaranteed affordability.

HSAs in the Workplace

People are going to have to start paying a lot more attention to their health insurance, even if it's provided by their employer. "The government is finding more ways for us to pay for our health costs," reported Deena Katz. "One big way is the health savings account."

Katz predicts HSAs will be adopted very quickly by companies stretched by insurance costs; the companies would fully or partially fund a worker's HSA and then be able to offer a cheaper high-deductible policy with a smaller hit to the company's budget. She believes that corporations may even simply fund a worker's HSA and then let the worker purchase his or her own HSA-eligible catastrophic insurance policy with the money, although there is some question as to whether the current law would allow this. "Health insurance is extremely expensive for employers," she said. "I'm an employer, and my health insurance costs have gone up thirty-five percent a year for the last three years. We're all feeling the crunch. One of the ways the government has tried to attack this problem is to put HSAs in place. I think employers will be looking at them as a way to cap their spending or contain costs. They have tried HMOs [discussed in the next section], which haven't worked very well. I as an employer will say to an employee: 'I'm giving you three hundred dollars a month and putting it in your HSA. You have to go out and buy your insurance and use that money to pay the premiums and the deductible on it. The policy belongs to you. It's not linked to your work. If you leave the job, you can keep the insurance.'" Given the mobility of today's workers, portable insurance may be a good idea—especially if it doesn't shift too many expenses to the employee.

Hurley believes companies will first offer HSAs *and* a high-deductible policy to their employees. "It's OK to use HSA money to pay for COBRA and long-term-care policies," he said, "but not for general heath insurance premiums—at least for now. I really think the government wants to maintain the employer-employee relationship in terms of health care." He added, however, that this was "somewhat of a gray area" in the law and that some legal experts think the HSA language might actually allow employers to fund

HSAs and offer no other health insurance. This, of course, would mean the employee could then use an HSA to pay for premiums on an HSA-eligible policy, as Katz suggests.

Katz added: "No matter how you cut it, costs are going to shift from employer to employee. Health insurance is the biggie, and the older you get the more important it is.

A Look at Some Plans

For comparison purposes, eHealthInsurance—the online health insurance broker—provided some quotes on monthly premiums for three kinds of health insurance policies in a sampling of U.S. cities. For the data to be meaningful, you need to be familiar with the following terms:

- A *Fee-for-service (indemnity) plan* is the traditional kind of health-care policy that allows you to go to any doctor or hospital you choose. The plan usually has a relatively small annual deductible, typically $300, and pays 80 percent of the bill after that; the other 20 percent is your responsibility. There is an out-of-pocket maximum that can vary, but it generally hovers around $2,000. After you spend that amount of your own money, the policy pays 100 percent of your medical expenses. Fee-for-service is the most expensive health insurance you can buy.
- An *HMO (health maintenance organization)* is essentially a prepaid health plan. For a monthly premium, the HMO provides comprehensive care usually with no deductibles and few copayments. You are, however, limited in your choice of doctors, hospitals, and other health-care providers; they must be under contract with the HMO. You commonly must get a referral from your primary-care physician to see a specialist; if you don't, your treatment with the specialist is not covered. HMOs have been the source of many consumer complaints

over the years, often over denial of expensive services. HMOs, however, can be among the least expensive health-insurance options depending on the state and coverage.

- A *PPO (preferred provider organization)* is a cross between fee-for-service and an HMO. You can see doctors outside the network, although you may be reimbursed for your expenses at a lower rate. For network doctors, you usually have a copayment for office visits. There can be varying deductibles and co-payments, along with out-of-pocket maximums, depending on the policy. You do not need a referral to see a specialist or any other doctor. In some states PPOs can be cheaper than HMOs. A PPO is the kind of policy that is most commonly made HSA-eligible by adding a high deductible.
- A *POS (point-of-service) plan* is like a PPO except that you need a referral from your primary-care physician to see an out-of-network doctor. Without the referral, you may have to pay the entire doctor's bill.

The quotes from eHealthInsurance are for the least expensive premiums in five states (and five specific cities) for HMO, PPO, and HSA-eligible policies. These quotes cover four sets of people: two married thirty-five-year-old adults with two children, ages five and eight; two married forty-eight-year-old adults with no children; a single forty-year-old male; and a single forty-year-old female. In each case, the premium quotes assume the policyholders live in the following cities: Springfield, New Jersey; San Jose, California; Chicago, Illinois; Phoenix, Arizona; and Atlanta, Georgia. Note that one of these states, New Jersey, has both guaranteed-issue laws and community rating; it is a state in which HSA-eligible policies are not yet available. Annual out-of-pocket maximums vary but are generally between $2,000 and $4,000, except in New Jersey, where the out-of-pocket maximum on the PPO plans is $10,000. Also keep in mind that the HSA-eligible plans' out-of-pocket maximums are set by law: $5,000 for an individual and $10,000 for a family. The deductibles on the HSA-eligible policies are, of course, much larger than for the other plans and are generally equal to the maximum amounts that may be contributed annually to a health savings account: $2,600 for an individual and $5,150 for a family.

For the thirty-five-year-old couple with children, here are the monthly premiums for an HMO, a PPO, and an HSA-eligible plan:

	HMO	PPO	HSA-Eligible
Springfield	$1,161.96	$1,433.38	N.A.
San Jose	$1,020.64	$261.00	$238.00
Chicago*	$1,124.12	$549.97	$201.00
Phoenix	$421.00	$373.46	$197.00
Atlanta	$776.00	$556.00	$296.10

*At the time of publication, ehealthinsurance did not offer HMO plans in Chicago, so the HMO price there reflects a PPO plan with no deductible and no copayment.

Here are the premiums on these three plans for the forty-eight-year-old couple with no children:

	HMO	PPO	HSA-Eligible
Springfield	$820.53	$1,005.88	N.A.
San Jose	$855.09	$318.00	$235.00
Chicago*	$1,048.52	$475.33	$173.00
Phoenix	$395.00	$374.49	$224.17
Atlanta	$512.00	$591.83	$324.30

*At the time of publication, ehealthinsurance did not offer HMO plans in Chicago, so the HMO price there reflects a PPO plan with no deductible and no copayment.

For the single forty-year-old male:

	HMO	PPO	HSA-Eligible
Springfield	$383.67	$502.94	N.A.
San Jose	$422.00	$133.00	$100.00
Chicago*	$397.30	$212.39	$143.67
Phoenix	$135.00	$119.89	$88.84
Atlanta	$177.00	$189.21	$129.25

*At the time of publication, ehealthinsurance did not offer HMO plans in Chicago, so the HMO price there reflects a PPO plan with no deductible and no copayment.

And for the single forty-year-old female:

	HMO	PPO	HSA-Eligible
Springfield	$383.67	$502.94	N.A.
San Jose	$422.00	$133.00	$100.00
Chicago*	$460.87	$246.37	$165.16
Phoenix	$195.00	$172.45	$102.12
Atlanta	$279.00	$272.58	$148.05

*At the time of publication, ehealthinsurance did not offer HMO plans in Chicago, so the HMO price there reflects a PPO plan with no deductible and no copayment.

You can view all the details on these plans and others of your choosing at eHealthInsurance's Web site. By the time this book is published, many of the premiums will probably have changed. The relative difference among them, however, is what's important.

As is clear from the preceding examples, these HSA-eligible policies, despite the high deductibles, will save you money on premiums—sometimes a lot. There appears to be little question that this new kind of insurance policy can make a dent in the enormous number of people without health insurance. According to Gary Lauer, the chief executive of eHealthInsurance, almost a third of HSA plans purchased through his company are bought by people who were previously uninsured; 46 percent were purchased by individuals and families with incomes of $50,000 or less. He also said that 6 percent of HSA plans were purchased by people forty years old and up; 62 percent were purchased by families and 38 percent by individuals. "These are policies with comprehensive benefits after deductibles are met," he added.

eHealthInsurance published an advertising booklet that explains the details of HSA plans and gives examples of possible savings. One example is a couple in their midthirties, with two grade-school-age children, living in San Diego, California. A typical fee-for-service health insurance plan for them with a $500 annual deductible would cost $9,936 a year.

Now assume the family bought an HSA-eligible plan with an annual premium of only $2,712, but with a deductible of $4,800. That means they can make a tax-free contribution to the HSA for up to the amount of the deductible. Using a federal tax rate of 25 percent and a state tax rate of 9 percent, the family will save $1,632 on taxes. If the HSA plan's annual premium and the HSA contribution are subtracted from the $9,936 that the traditional plan cost, that would provide additional savings of $2,424 per year. What they save on taxes and premiums—$4,056—is only $744 short of the amount they need to fund their HSA.

For any medical bills, however, they will first have to spend $4,800 in a given year out of their HSA; only then will their insurance kick in. Depending on their policy, they still could face some copayment costs. However, by law, their maximum out-of-pocket annual expenses are $10,000. If they have no big expense for two or three years, their HSA—growing at the rate of $4,800 a year—would easily cover that maximum. Keep in mind that they can keep that part of the HSA they don't spend on health care, but they can't spend it on anything else or they will have to pay taxes plus a 10 percent penalty on it. At the age of sixty-five, when they are eligible for Medicare, the couple can withdraw the money without penalty and spend it on anything they want, although they must pay taxes (but no penalty) on it. Even after age sixty-five, the money is tax-free if they use it for medical expenses. How much money are we talking about? It depends on how much they spend each year on medical care. The example assumes they spend $2,000 a year and leave $2,800 in the account. After thirty years, with a 4 percent return, they would have $162,484. Is $2,000 a year a reasonable amount to expect a family of four to spend for health care? Maybe, maybe not; some years they might spend more, some years less. According to the most recent government figures, the average medical expenses in the United States are $2,700 a year per person; the mean is $720 per person. Even if the family has to use all the money in the HSA, however, they will still have spent less on health insurance. In addition, they, not an HMO, will control which doctors they see and what treatments they get.

Know the Territory

Health insurance in the United States is complicated, tricky, and expensive. No article or book chapter can do more than scratch the surface. You need to get to know the rules and the laws in your state. Compare prices and details on the Internet. Before signing on the dotted line for any insurance, ask this question: What does this policy *not* cover? Sometimes the answer to that can be as important as a list of what is covered.

An insurance broker like eHealthInsurance can be helpful, as can a regular offline broker in your area. Independent financial counselors can also be of assistance. They often can tell you which companies have reputations for increasing premiums, for making it difficult to file claims, or for delaying payments. The National Association of Health Underwriters (www.nahu.org) can help you find one of their members in your area.

6

Education: Costs vs. Rewards

I refuse to sacrifice for you and then resent you for it.

— ORSON BEAN

In a television appearance on *The Merv Griffin Show* in the early 1970s, the actor Orson Bean—during what he now refers to as his "hippie-actor-eccentric-adventures period"—was asked if he was saving money to send his children to college. His answer was no. He said he had told his kids that he was using the money now and that when the time came for them to go to college, he'd be happy to give them whatever money he had at the time. If he had none, he continued, they would have to fend for their own education.

In a 1977 op-ed article in the *New York Times* titled "Ready to Face Tomorrow," Bean explained his stance: "We've used all the money we have lovingly put away for the kids' college education. If we have enough when they are ready for college . . . years from now, we will happily give it to them. If we don't, they can get a scholarship or work their way through. Or not go at all—I'm not dedicated to the proposition that everyone has to go to college anyway." He continued: "I am dedicated to giving my kids the memory of happy parents. So I spend a lot of time with them. We really know each other. If they should decide later on that they hate me, at least they'll know who they're hating."

In a 2004 interview for this book, Bean, who is now seventy-six, reflected on his past comments and stood by them. "What I was saying about my kids on the *Griffin* show was this: I refuse to sacrifice for you and then resent you for it," he declared. His two sons and two daughters eventually all went to college, and with his help. "I had the dough when the time came," he said. "I just hadn't put it away. I didn't in the least strap myself for a long period of time to pay for their education, to send them to schools they may not have wanted to go to or that they may not have been able to get into."

Spending the money he had saved for college expenses was the result of a period of life reassessment he went through in the late 1960s and early 1970s. "We took off and went to Australia for a year and a half," he explained. "I gave up my career and then came back and resumed it in a half-assed way. That's when I bought a van and began dragging my poor long-suffering family around the country."

He also canceled his life insurance. "To me, life is a gamble," he said. "I decided a long time ago to gamble on the positive side. I decided to gamble that I wouldn't get sick and die but live well and happy into my hundreds."

He has no regrets. "I'm having a wonderful time. I made the discovery that it's always now. It's now, and three seconds from now is still now. The now that I mentioned three seconds ago is what we call the past. When I realized that, I said I'm not putting any money aside for this nonexistent future, which is just a figment of our imagination. People say to me, 'What if?' Well, the other side of 'What if?' is that on my seventy-fifth birthday I took twenty people—my extended family—to Club Med in Mexico for a week. I started my seventy-fifth birthday standing in warm Mexican water with a piña colada in one hand, a grandchild in the other. I wouldn't have been able to do that if I'd been worrying about saving for college or paying off those college bills. Anyway, I have a long-standing suspicion of intellectuals. I hope my grandkids don't go to college. I'd rather give them money to spend a couple of years traveling around the world."

DON'T SACRIFICE FUTURE SECURITY

While Orson Bean's unconventional approach to higher education and paying for it might not be for everyone, there is a lesson to be learned from his approach: many people stretch themselves too thin financially in order to send their children to expensive and prestigious schools where costs, including room and board, can run more than $40,000 a year. The expense, and the havoc it can wreak on parents' future security, may not always be worth it.

In a *Los Angeles Times* financial advice column written in 2004, Liz Pulliam Weston featured a letter from a reader asking if there was anything wrong with using IRA money to pay for his children's college if the money were replaced once the children graduated. Weston warned the reader against the idea: "Your kids can get through school with loans, part-time jobs, and perhaps some financial aid. Would you rather try to borrow to get through retirement?"

Peter Wall is a financial adviser and a senior vice president at Chase Investment Services. The group he heads at Chase advises clients on comprehensive financial planning, including providing for their children's education. Wall said that people usually have to juggle several financial priorities, and for his clients these priorities tend to be, in order of importance: saving for retirement, saving for children's education, and helping provide for their parents. They also have to cope with higher college costs and with their parents living longer, "plus, they have fewer defined-benefit pension plans, and many haven't saved enough," he added. "They're making more money than their parents ever dreamed, yet they're finding themselves in situations where they are overextended by these three priorities. I think mortgaging your future and endangering your retirement to send a child to a fancy, expensive school is a terribly unfair position to put yourself in, or to put your kids in. No one wants to be in a situation later in life when you're retired and living on really limited means. Or wind up with your children having to support you if you have overextended yourself."

Wall and his colleagues at Chase estimate that the average cost of tuition, fees, and room and board at a four-year private college is $26,854; for a public university, it's $10,636. They assume increases of 5 percent a year. These are, of course, only averages. Many top-flight private schools run much more than that. In July 2004, the Associated Press reported that the members of the National Association of Independent Colleges and Universities would increase tuition alone by an average of 6 percent for the 2004–5 school year, to just over $18,000. Private institutions account for about half of American colleges and educate about 20 percent of four-year college students, according to the AP.

Many students save money by attending a community college for two years and then finishing at a four-year college. The savings can be hefty: according to the College Board, the average annual community college tuition for the 2003–4 school years was $1,905. In addition, community college students usually save additional money by living at home.

The high prices of some colleges and universities can, Wall contends, result in unfair pressure on a child to come out of college and find a position that will justify all the money that was spent. "A colleague of mine sends his son to a school that costs more than thirty-five thousand dollars a year," he said. "His son has elected to major in history and go into high school teaching, which he loves. The ripple through the family when he declared his major was pretty significant. The response was: 'Why are you going to such an expensive school to become a teacher? You could have gone to a cheaper school because you're never going to justify the investment we're making.' Now this boy is reconsidering what he should do for a career. He could end up in a career in which he is unhappy. Unfortunately, they put the cart before the horse. You can't really blame the boy; he made a choice on what he wants to do, but he was at a school that was costing his parents more than they could really afford. So there was a lot of pressure on him because of that. That can make for some unhappy lives. It's tough to ask kids to make decisions so early about what they want to do with their lives."

The pressure to attend this kind of school ultimately comes from the parents. "There can be a lot of peer pressure among kids, but that also comes from the parents who see sending their kids to a top school as prestigious," Wall said. "A level of pride and status goes with saying that my kid is smart enough to go to such and such a school, and I can afford it. Sometimes they can't afford it, but they pretend they can. Or maybe they can afford it but the money is going from the retirement pocket to the college pocket. They say, 'I'll spend forty thousand for college and worry about my retirement later.' Well, that's four years of investment and returns that are missed, more if there are two or three children involved." Or, as Orson Bean makes clear, the money may also come from that needed for current living expenses. This can create a dilemma: Should you mortgage your retirement future or reduce your standard of living?

Wall's advice to middle-income parents and students: "Lighten up, look at less expensive options. In the end, where you go to school is not that important. It's the individual, not the school, that will be the biggest part of success, however you define it. If you go to a good school that provides a good, basic education and you make the most of that, it's not important that the school have a prestigious name attached to it. And the parents will still have some money left for retirement."

Wall stressed the importance of picking the right school. "You want a school that offers the most bang for your buck. Costs and reputation are not necessarily the key things you need to consider about a school. My personal observation is that if there is an advantage to going to, for instance, an Ivy League school, it may be the networking opportunities it offers. These kinds of opportunities are probably better than at lower-echelon schools like state universities." The extent of these networking opportunities, of course, depends partly on a student's field of study and how effectively he or she takes advantage of them.

Wall cited the case of his son: "As I've told my seventeen-year-old son, if you apply yourself to school and focus on what you're doing, commit to it, and come out with good grades and good contacts with professors and other faculty members, you're going to do well no matter where you go. You'll have the references, the grades, and the education; you'll be fine. If you have strong interpersonal skills, you'll do fine. You don't need a pedigree diploma to get your foot in the door. I also told him not to think that just because you get accepted to an Ivy League school and attend it, that your road will be paved with good fortune. It's not going to guarantee you a job or an income. That will come from your own applications and your own hard work. My brother, for instance, went to Rutgers University and is now a federal judge. When I was at his swearing-in ceremony, I looked around at some of the other judges. Most had gone to fairly prestigious schools. I told my son that it just goes to show that you don't have to go to Harvard and Yale to succeed. His uncle is an example."

That's pretty good advice from a father to a son, and, as a result, the younger Wall, an honor student, is applying to a mix of schools and is keeping his options open.

Any big bookstore has a section full of books offering advice on selecting a college. Their value and quality vary greatly. One that I like is *Harvard Schmarvard: Getting Beyond the Ivy League to the College That Is Best for You* (Three Rivers Press, 2003) by Jay Mathews, an education reporter and columnist for the *Washington Post*. It is practical and takes a refreshingly contrarian approach to high-profile schools. One of the book's best features is an appendix titled "Hidden Gems" that lists 100 colleges that the author says are "better than you think."

SO WHERE'S THE PAYOFF?

People who insist their children go to big-name schools often fall back on the argument that, yes, such schools are expensive, but graduates—with their prestigious degrees—will earn more in the workplace than those who graduated from lesser-known colleges and universities.

There's only one problem with this argument: it's not true.

Alan B. Krueger, the Bendheim Professor of Economics and Public Affairs at Princeton University, and Stacy Berg Dale, a researcher at Mathematica Policy Research, released a study in 2000 that reviewed earnings after almost twenty years of two groups of people who started college in 1976. The researchers looked at 6,335 sets of male students with identical Scholastic Aptitude Test scores who were accepted at the same types of colleges. Some students in each set graduated from a top college, like those in the Ivy League; others, whose SAT scores were good enough to get into Harvard or Yale, elected to go to a state university or other less selective college.

The somewhat surprising results: in 1995, the latter group of students had a slightly higher average salary—$91,232 a year—than their peers who attended selective schools, whose annual salaries averaged $90,144. In other words, for students of comparable ability and choices, the selectivity of the colleges they attended made almost no difference in future earnings (see figure 7). Similar results were found for women.

The study, however, did show that students from lower-income families who attended selective schools did see a benefit in earnings. Their annual income was $73,500, compared with $67,790 for students from lower-income families who went to less selective schools. In Krueger's view, this was probably because of the contacts such students were able to make at select schools. "These students gain the most from going to elite schools, but they are the ones elite schools are least likely to admit," he said in an interview for this book. The increased earnings for a lower-income student, however, must be weighed against the much higher costs of attending a select school. It's one thing if financial aid is available, another if a student and family are trying to foot the full bill and, perhaps, taking on a lot of debt.

In an April 27, 2000, column in the *New York Times* in which he discussed the study, Krueger had the following advice for students: "Don't believe that the only school worth attending is one that would not admit you. That you go to college is more important than where you go. Find a school whose academic strengths match your interests and which devotes resources to instruction in those fields. Recognize that your own motivation, ambition, and talents will determine your success more than the college name on your diploma."

Figure 7

Alma Mater and Income Later

Average annual earnings in 1995 for workers who enrolled as freshmen in 1976:

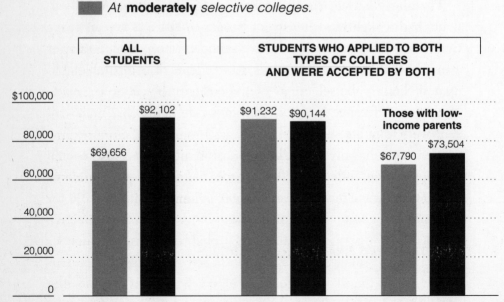

Source: Alan B. Krueger

His advice to elite colleges: "Recognize that the most disadvantaged students benefit most from your instruction. Set financial aid and admission policies accordingly."

During his interview, Krueger added that parents and students should consider not just a school's reputation but what the school puts into a student's education. "All the elite schools don't necessarily put in the same amount," he said. "Just because a school is selective and hard to get into and considered elite doesn't necessarily mean it's going to raise your child's earnings power. Some colleges have a great reputation, but the best professors are hardly ever in the classroom. They have an ethic that professors don't spend much time with students. There are other schools that are less prestigious but where faculty members spend a lot of time with students. Being elite and providing a lot of resources are not necessarily the same. Also, some schools are good in some departments and not in others. Harvard's a great school, but if your child wants to be an engineer it's not great in engineering. What is really important is that parents not make a rigid decision and say that the most expensive school has got to be the best. That's just not the case for all students."

Krueger agrees that the study certainly lends support to the notion that parents ought to think twice about sending their children to an elite school if it's going to put their financial security or retirement plans at risk. He suggested that parents in this situation should consider sending their children to a less expensive undergraduate school and then, if they do well there, to a more prestigious graduate school. "At the graduate level, more assistance is usually available," he said. "Students will be able to help themselves more than they could when they were eighteen."

"WE DID WHAT WAS FINANCIALLY RESPONSIBLE FOR OUR FAMILY"

Jim and Elizabeth Hammond of Columbia, South Carolina, have two children—Thomas and Sarah—one in college, the other in graduate school. Neither child has incurred any debt, and the parents have not had to tap their retirement savings to pay for schooling.

Sarah Hammond was the valedictorian of her class when she graduated from high school in 1998 in Columbia, where her father was the state capital correspondent for the *Greenville News*. She wanted to be a writer and was accepted by the University of South Carolina, the University of Pennsylvania, Furman University, the University of North Carolina at Chapel Hill, and the University of Virginia.

Sarah wanted to go to the University of Pennsylvania because of its prestige as an Ivy League school. At the time, it would have cost about $35,000 a year. However, she was offered a full four-year scholarship, including money for room and board, at the University of South Carolina. Jim wanted her to accept the South Carolina offer.

In the end, Sarah agreed to attend the University of South Carolina, where she graduated magna cum laude in 2002 with a degree in English. She is now enrolled in a three-year master's degree program for playwrights at the University of Iowa in Iowa City. Three of her plays—*Kudzu, Wax Work*, and *Green Girl*—have already been professionally produced in South Carolina and Iowa. She is pursuing a career as a playwright.

Thomas is a junior at the University of South Carolina, where he is majoring in music. He won a merit scholarship that pays more than a third of his annual college costs of around $14,000.

Jim, who now works as a political consultant, estimated that if Sarah had gone to the University of Pennsylvania, her four years there would have cost the family $140,000. "We would have had to borrow money," he said. "As it was, we had some money invested in a second home—a beach home—that we did not have to sell to help pay for college. That house's value increased dramatically during the four years Sarah was in college. We were then able to sell it and pay off our primary home mortgage. We bought the beach house when she started high school, and we agreed we would sell it if we needed the money to pay for her college. But we didn't have to. The net effect of Sarah going to the University of South Carolina rather than the University of Pennsylvania was that the value of our assets continued to grow, we were able to pay our house off, and she graduated from college with no debt."

Even without her scholarship, Jim said Sarah's college costs for four years at South Carolina would have been less than $40,000.

The Hammonds took the course recommended by Krueger. "In exchange for Sarah agreeing to go to South Carolina, we agreed to subsidize her for whatever graduate school she wanted to go to," Jim said. Her costs at the University of Iowa, which is one of the top schools for writers in the country, run about $20,000 a year. The Hammonds pay half; Sarah pays the other half with some scholarship funds and money that she earns working as a teaching assistant.

Jim added: "To me, the benefit of graduating from college with no debt, for the family or the graduate, is incalculable. We will end up having put two kids through college, and nobody will owe anything. Plus, we paid the mortgage on our house. When I was in college, I worked every semester and finished with debt, which is still the case for many students. I never got to fully participate in the academic and social life of college because I had to work. Sarah worked some, but it was work of her choice. She didn't have to. She had every opportunity to fully partake of the college experience.

"We wanted to make sure our kids got good educations. Sarah got a good education at the University of South Carolina, and Thomas is getting a good education. We did what was financially responsible for our family."

Sarah says that in the end she was happy with the decision. "I know I got a good education at USC," she said. "I also know, though, that I am lacking some of the connections and some of the immediate brand-name prestige. That's the stuff that people pay for when they go to those schools. I don't feel slighted, but I do wonder what would have been the difference."

She said when she graduated from high school she had wanted to go away to college. "At the time, it seemed awful to stay in my hometown—even though I wasn't living at home—when everyone else was going away to school. It was difficult at the time to make that adjustment."

She has also come to appreciate the money she and her parents saved. "I understand things better now," she said. "If it had been my decision alone, I would have gone to the University of Pennsylvania and ended up in terrible, terrible debt—which I am extremely glad I'm not. Being in grad school with others who have had to put themselves through school has helped me see the importance of the money angle. Now I'm teaching students who miss my classes because they have to work. Some of them have to support their parents. That really hits home for me and makes me realize what a good deal I got."

In the end, perhaps the best way to cope with college expenses is a blend of the approaches taken by Orson Bean, Peter Wall, and the Hammond family.

Saving is important, and the more the better—but don't save so much of your income that you end up with a lifestyle that is too sparse or forces you to live on the financial edge. To paraphrase Bean, things have a way of working out. When the time comes for a student to go to college, consider the alternatives in terms of the money available, and the financial aid the student can get or money he or she can earn. Don't be too dogmatic or obsessive about a prestige private college or university. If money has to be borrowed, let the student obtain the loan. Above all, don't put your retirement in jeopardy to send a child to college. There are too many other ways, as the Hammond family showed.

Just because you've saved a certain amount for college expenses doesn't mean you have to spend all of it if there are less expensive alternatives. The Hammonds, remember, were prepared to sell their beach house to send their daughter to an Ivy League school. Instead they were able to sell the house and pay off their primary residence—a move that effectively increased their income. That's a neat trick to pull off with two kids in college.

7

Cars: A Money Pit

If you get the feeling you're being hustled when
you walk into a car dealership, it's because you are.

—GARY DOBBINS, INDEPENDENT AUTO BROKER

If you're serious about saving money, look no farther than your driveway. Take a hard look at your car or cars; they are a serious source of expenses for many people, sometimes ranking just behind housing. Like credit cards, they are an essential part of life for most people, and, like credit cards, you must get them under control.

First, consider getting by with just one car. This can be difficult for working couples or for families with several drivers, but the savings are significant. When you sell one of your automobiles, not only do you eliminate a car or lease payment, or free up some money if you paid cash for the vehicle, but you also greatly reduce your auto insurance bills, which in some high-cost cities and states are considerable.

When the time comes to replace that car, should you buy a new or used one? In most cases, the most expensive thing you can do is buy or lease a new car every two or three years. The least expensive route is to purchase a used car, especially one that is coming off lease and may still be under warranty. There is also a middle way: buy a new car and run it until it dies.

THAT FIRST YEAR IS EXPENSIVE

The problem with a new car is that its depreciation, or decline in value, is much higher during the early life of the vehicle—especially during the first year. Buying a used car, or keeping a new car for a long time, allows you to avoid much of that depreciation or minimize it by spreading it out over many years, perhaps ten to twelve. Of course, if you do get a new car every two or three years, repair costs are reduced because your car is always under warranty. As you will see, however, this is a very minor plus compared with the negative of depreciation.

The rapid depreciation of a new car can be a nasty problem if you financed the vehicle for five years or more, paid little or no money down, and want to sell or trade the car before the loan is paid off—say in two or three years. You will likely discover that you will still owe more on the car than it's worth.

Gary Dobbins is an independent automobile broker in Chadds Ford, Pennsylvania. He arranges leases and purchases of cars, new and used, for his clients. He argues that the greatest financial advantage can be gained by buying a late-model used car. He cites the case of a 2004 Volvo, with a $34,000 sticker price, that he leased to a couple in late 2003. After eight months, they decided they needed a van. (Luckily, their lease was structured so that they could get out of it easily.) Dobbins, whose company is called Dobbins Auto-smarts, then sold the used Volvo, which had only 6,000 miles on it, to another client for $24,000—a full $10,000 under the original price. "That car was a great deal," he said. "It still had three and a half years of the manufacturer's warranty left and had already taken the big depreciation hit."

If you want further proof of how expensive owning a new car can be, or how much you can save with a used car, visit the www.Edmunds.com Web site. Once there, click on "True Own-ership Costs" on the home page, which will take you to the "True Cost to Own," or "TCO," section. You'll be able to select a car model and see the estimated costs of ownership for five years, de-pending on the state in which you live. You can also, with some minimum calculations, see the advantage of buying a late-model used car.

Take, for instance, a 2004 Chevrolet Malibu LS four-door sedan with a 3.5-liter six-cylinder engine. According to Edmunds, the esti-mated new-car purchase price in New Jersey would be $22,069, in-cluding the state's sales taxes and fees totaling $1,325. (The price of the car without the taxes and fees would be $20,744, a number that will be useful in some later calculations.)

The true cost of owning that Malibu for five years—the TCO—would be $35,073. That includes depreciation, financing, insurance, taxes and fees, fuel, maintenance, and repairs. That works out to an average per-mile cost of 47 cents over the five-year period. (The In-ternal Revenue Service, however, allows you to deduct only 36 cents a mile when the use of your car is a tax-deductible expense; many companies use the IRS figure to reimburse employees who use their cars for company business.)

Let's look more closely at four of the expense elements and the assumptions behind them in the Edmunds calculations: deprecia-tion, financing, maintenance, and repairs.

- *Depreciation* is the amount by which a car declines in value from its purchase price. As we saw with the Dobbins Volvo, most depreciation takes place early on, during the first year. In calculating depreciation and resale values, Edmunds assumes that you will drive the car 15,000 miles a year, keep it in "clean" condition, and sell it to a private party. If you sell the car to a dealer or use it as a trade-in, its value would almost cer-tainly be lower.

- *Financing* is the interest expense on a car loan. Edmunds assumes a good credit rating, a down payment of 10 percent, and a loan term of sixty months, or five years. Edmunds is able to constantly update its Web site to account for the slightest changes in interest rates for loans—and fuel prices—which I obviously can't do here. If you go to the Edmunds Web site, you will get a different number for interest charges, fuel costs, and the True Cost to Own, depending on current rates and prices. Financing charges are typically based on the balance due and will decrease over the five years as that balance declines.
- *Maintenance* includes work that needs to be done to your car on a regular basis, like oil changes. It also includes unscheduled items like replacing batteries, brakes, hoses, mufflers, lights, and so on. As you might expect, maintenance will increase as your car ages.
- *Repairs* refer to work that must be done on your car that is not covered by the manufacturer's warranty. Older cars typically require more repairs.

Putting all the cost elements together, figure 8 shows how Edmunds comes up with the $35,073 that it costs to own a $22,069 car. Depreciation is the killer. While Edmunds rates the operating costs of that specific model as average, its depreciation is above average. In fact, the car's value plummets by $8,461 in the first year alone. By the fifth year, its value will drop by only $1,312. Maintenance and repairs will rise as the car ages and depreciation drops, but it's not an even match—not even close.

As figure 8 clearly shows—and as Gary Dobbins demonstrated with his Volvo—you can save a lot money on a car if you can avoid that first year of depreciation. Let's assume, for instance, that instead of buying the Malibu new, you buy it when it is three years old. Edmunds estimates its resale value at $8,759 (the purchase

Figure 8

Costs of Owning a Typical New Sedan

Some costs, like maintenance and repair, rise as a car gets older. Others are much higher when a car is new, like depreciation and taxes. Assuming steady use and a clean driving record, fuel and insurance costs rise gradually with inflation.

	First year	Second year	Third year	Fourth year	Fifth year	Total over five years
Depreciation	$ 8,461	$ 1,874	$ 1,650	$ 1,462	$ 1,312	**$ 14,759**
Repairs	0	0	99	237	344	**680**
Maintenance	320	473	390	809	1,037	**3,029**
Taxes and fees	1,325	49	36	36	36	**1,482**
Financing	868	694	511	318	114	**2,505**
Insurance	1,243	1,287	1,332	1,379	1,427	**6,668**
Fuel	1,120	1,154	1,189	1,225	1,262	**5,950**
Total	$ 13,337	$ 5,531	$ 5,207	$ 5,466	$ 5,532	**$ 35,073**

Source: Edmunds.com

price of the car, without sales tax or fees, minus three years' depreciation). The car would only have 45,000 miles on it, and the bulk of the expenses of depreciation would have hit the car's previous owner, greatly decreasing the per-mile costs. If the car were five years old, with 75,000 miles on it, you could pick it up for $5,985. By then the depreciation would have tapered way off and the per-mile costs would be even less. Most modern cars can easily go 100,000 miles or more without serious mechanical problems. If you buy the car with 75,000 on it, you can reasonably expect to drive it another 30,000 miles, or two years, without a serious breakdown. The price of that five-year-old car, $5,985, that you are going to drive for two years, or perhaps longer, is $4,350 *less than the depreciation alone on a new Malibu for just the first two years!*

If you drive that five-year-old car longer than two years, the per-mile cost gets less and less the longer you drive it—but only to a point. That point is when the cost of repairs gets too expensive. The trick is to know when to stop. One rule of thumb is to give up the car when your annual repair costs equal what annual car payments on a comparable new car would be. I think that's even a little high; it ignores the inconvenience of getting a car fixed. I would put the breaking point at slightly more than half of annual car payments. The point is to live well and save money. Spending too much time waiting for my car to get fixed is not my idea of living well.

If you want an even more dramatic example of how your car-buying habits can limit your financial future, consider an expensive—and expensive to operate—sport utility vehicle like the Ford Expedition. Let's use the top-of-the-line Eddie Bauer model with four-wheel drive and a 5.4-liter V-8 engine. The total cost of the vehicle purchased in New Jersey is $40,613. The True Cost to Own over five years, however, is $56,972. That works out to 76 cents a mile. As figure 9 shows, this vehicle depreciates by almost $12,000 during just the first year. The fuel costs alone for five years are more than $10,000.

"PEOPLE CAN BE VERY EASILY MISLED."

Dobbins became an independent auto broker about twelve years ago because he had become disillusioned with the traditional dealership-centered business, where he had worked since the early 1970s. He had started as a salesman and worked his way up to business manager at a large dealership that sold vehicles for eleven manufacturers. "I didn't like the way I saw customers being treated," he said. "So I walked away from it and went to the customer's side as a broker."

Dobbins acts as the customer's agent—getting the best deal he can, arranging financing, doing all the paperwork, and in most cases delivering the car to his client's house. His customers get a car in a relatively hassle-free way, never having to set foot inside an auto dealership or deal with a salesperson. (Full disclosure: my

Figure 9

Costs of Owning a Top-of-the-Line SUV

Sport utility vehicles do not just cost more to buy, on average, than passenger cars — they are also more expensive to own and operate after purchase. Compare these figures with those in Figure 8 for a new sedan.

	First year	Second year	Third year	Fourth year	Fifth year	Total over five years
Depreciation	$11,942	$ 3,831	$ 3,371	$ 2,988	$ 2,683	**$ 24,815**
Repairs	0	0	109	258	375	**742**
Maintenance	661	951	1,098	1,791	1,220	**5,721**
Taxes and fees	2,624	74	61	61	61	**2,881**
Financing	1,800	1,439	1,059	659	237	**5,194**
Insurance	1,359	1,407	1,456	1,507	1,560	**7,289**
Fuel	1,946	2,004	2,064	2,126	2,190	**10,330**
Total	$ 20,332	$ 9,706	$ 9,218	$ 9,390	$ 8,326	**$ 56,972**

Source: Edmunds.com

wife and I have bought or leased three cars from Dobbins over the last decade.)

"If you get the feeling you're being hustled when you walk into a car dealership, it's because you are," Dobbins said. "And a lot of people feel that way. It's because salesmen at dealerships are trained that if you don't sell people the day they walk in the door, the odds of seeing them again are very slim. That's the approach sellers take. They'll do whatever is possible to sell you a car that day. They're pressured, and they put pressure on you, because they think if you don't buy then, you won't be back. Most of the time that's true. That's just the way people are when it comes to buying automobiles."

While Dobbins believes that a good salesperson "can talk someone into almost anything" and that "people can be very easily misled," he said buyers are increasingly doing their homework before making a purchase. "They can find so much more information online that wasn't available a few years ago," he noted. "The fact that people have more information is one reason the automobile business is so totally different now, so competitive."

All this competition translates into lower profits for car dealers, and that in turn helps trigger more high-pressure selling. "A dealer's profit on a new car is much lower than it used to be," Dobbins said. "That's a big change. A dealer can sell a thirty-thousand-dollar and make maybe four hundred dollars. That's a joke. They can't survive on that. Dealers now make more money on servicing and financing than on selling new cars. In fact, the bigger dealerships have really started concentrating on financing, where there is a lot of money to be made." This is why you see so many ads in which dealers push great financing deals—which often hold hidden expenses.

When I first got a car through Dobbins Autosmarts, I was concerned that getting warranty repairs might pose a problem since I would be taking the car to a dealer from whom I did not buy the car. This, in fact, turned out to be no problem whatsoever. Three cars later, I have never had even the slightest difficulty with such work at any dealer.

Dobbins explained why. "Good dealers separate their service and sales departments. They're happy to get warranty work from any source. They get paid well by the manufacturers for it. An automaker might allow, for instance, a dealer to bill twelve hours for a specific job. So the dealer gives it to their best mechanic, who can do the job in half that time. The dealer still gets paid for the twelve hours. I have dealership service departments in my area who call me and ask for my customers' business. . . . They say, 'Don't worry about them; we'll take good care of your customers no matter where they got the car.'"

In addition to buying and leasing cars for clients, Dobbins will buy specifically requested used cars at big auto auctions he goes to each week.

There's no question that using a broker like Dobbins is a low-stress, convenient way to get a car. But is it cheaper? Based on my experience and the experiences of others, the answer is yes. Dobbins says he can usually save a customer $1,000 on a new car. On a late-model used car, the savings can often be $2,000 to $3,000 over the price negotiated at a dealer's used-car lot. "I get new cars at good prices because I try to stick with one or two dealers for each kind of new car I sell," he said. "For a Honda dealer, for instance, I represent ten to fifteen sales a month. So I'm going to get their best price. The used cars I get at auction are often ones that have come off lease and are being sold by banks. It's amazing how much money can be saved on them."

Dobbins makes money on new cars by getting a small cut from the financing, typically 1 percent, and the difference, often a few hundred dollars, between what he actually pays for the car and the dealer invoice price. For used cars that he buys at auctions for customers, he usually charges a flat rate. For a $7,500 car, he charges the customer $500; for a $15,000 car, $750. For more expensive cars, he'll usually charge $1,000.

To find a broker like Dobbins in your area, check the Yellow Pages or the Internet, where you'll also find online brokers. Use a search engine like Google, and just type in "auto broker."

Of course, people aren't always rational when it comes to buying a car. We are influenced by things like advertising, fantasies, egos, jealousies, and past experiences—all of which may or may not be relevant or good for our budget. How else can you explain the popularity of Hummers in traffic-clogged cities like Los Angeles and New York? To save money, you should try to be as coldly rational as possible about your transportation needs. I once read an interview with a former executive of a fancy European carmaker who said that when you get down to it, any car is just "four wheels rolling down the road." A reporter friend of mine was amazed at the reply when he once asked a top American auto executive—off the record—what kind of car he would buy if his only concerns were value and quality. The executive's answer: a Toyota Camry.

One way to become more rational about buying a car is to do your homework before you enter a showroom. In addition to free Web sites like Edmunds.com, the one maintained by *Consumer Reports* magazine (www.ConsumerReports.org/cr/new22) will supply very useful information for a small fee. For twelve dollars, you can order a report, ten to twenty pages long, that will guide you through the process of buying or leasing a new car, arming you with specific information about dealer costs, rebates, and optional equipment. You can view your report online or have it delivered by fax or e-mail.

The report can actually save you a lot of legwork. Once you know the exact car you want and the price you're willing to pay, simply start calling dealers with your offer. Tell them they must accept or reject your offer over the phone, no haggling allowed. I once bought a new 1991 Saab that way. The sales manager at the third dealer I called accepted my offer, which was $500 above the dealer's price. "Just don't ask me to throw in free custom floor mats," she said. They would have cost another $100 or so.

BUYING FOR THE LONG HAUL

Despite the obvious advantages of buying a used car, some people just don't like the idea, even if a warranty is involved. I admit that I fall into that camp. It's not that I have anything against used cars per se; it's just that I have never had much luck buying them. I have friends, however, who do so frequently and often get fancy automobiles—BMWs and the like—for less than the price of a new subcompact.

I tend to favor the middle way: buying a new car and running it as long as possible. Although I do take the initial hit on depreciation, keeping the car long enough—ten years or so—will spread the loss over enough years so that it is much less painful than acquiring a new car every three years or so. Remember, most of the depreciation occurs during the first three years, and especially the first year, of owning a new car. The five-year depreciation total on the Malibu that we considered earlier is $14,759, with the drop in the fifth year being only $1,312. That total averages out to almost $3,000 a year. If you keep the car for ten years—and even assume that at that point it's worth zero—the per-year average falls to a little more than $2,000. It you keep it twelve years, that average declines to a bit more than $1,728. By keeping a car twelve years instead of three, you have cut the annual depreciation cost to $1,728 from $3,995!

With proper maintenance, keeping a car for ten years or more does not necessary mean big repair problems because cars built nowadays are so much better than in the past. If you don't think so, find a collector with a well-maintained 1955 model and check out its fit and finish. If the collector will let you, take it for a spin. You'll be happy to go back to the future.

While I have advocated—mainly because of the inconvenience factor—getting rid of an old car when the annual repairs become more than half the annual car payments for a comparable new car, there are people who recommend making major repairs and getting a second or third life out of a vehicle. Although it's not for everyone, this method of coping with transportation costs is not without its merits. Suppose you spend $5,000 to $7,000 to rebuild a car's engine and transmission plus other items that may need more than routine maintenance. That's pretty cheap compared with the $20,000 or more you'd probably spend for a new car. The rebuilt one will likely run nearly as long as a new one before it requires another round of major work.

Whatever your position on the car issue, there's no argument that cars are an expensive, if necessary, part of our modern lives. The most expensive way of all is to lease or buy a new car every two or three years. If that's been your practice, it's one of the easiest and most efficient places to start cutting expenses.

AUTO INSURANCE: THE HIGHS AND LOWS

A big part of the expense of owning a car is insurance. Like many other expenses, it varies widely around the United States, primarily because of accident and theft rates. To get a sense of the range of these insurance costs, let's consider the partial results of a study that were released early in 2004 by Runzheimer International, the management consulting firm based in Rochester, Wisconsin.

Runzheimer looked at the annual costs of insurance coverage for a new midsize sedan driven within a fifty-mile radius of a city. It used rates for both male and female drivers with clean driving records; the coverage included comprehensive, collision, bodily injury, property damage, and uninsured motorist coverage. The range was staggering, from almost $5,000 in Detroit, Michigan, to less than $1,000 in Nashville, Tennessee.

Here are the five most expensive cities:

Detroit	$4,945
Philadelphia	$3,666
Newark	$3,557
Los Angeles	$3,258
New York City	$2,762

The five least expensive cities were:

Nashville	$978
Boise, Idaho	$990
Richmond, Virginia	$1,038
Burlington, Vermont	$1,039
Evansville, Indiana	$1,045

"There's no mystery here," said David Freidlen, the product development director and vehicle costs expert for Runzheimer.

"Fewer accidents, vehicle thefts, and collision damage repair bills in Nashville versus Detroit translate into much lower annual insurance premiums."

An advantage to driving a car that is older than, say, four to six years, is that you can probably drop the collision coverage—and save a few hundred dollars a year—since the amount the insurance company will pay if you wreck the car is limited to its so-called book value. But remember, you'll be fully responsible for fixing your car or replacing it if it's totaled. Kelley Blue Book (www.kbb.com) is a good source of information on used auto values.

8

The Credit Card Game

I eventually just paid off in full so they didn't
get all that happy interest they wanted so badly.

—A CONSUMER'S COMMENT ON THE WWW.CARDRATINGS.COM WEB SITE

Henry Hamman, a consultant and faculty member at the University of Miami in Florida, wanted to sell a second home he and his wife owned in Colorado. Because of water damage, however, they first needed to do some repair work, including installing a new kitchen.

Hamman decided to play the credit card game to help finance the work.

He applied for and received a credit card from Lowe's with a $6,000 line of credit and another from Home Depot with a $10,000 credit line. Both cards carried a promotional offer of zero interest for a year on purchases of $299 or more. Essentially, Hamman got a free $16,000 loan to repair his house—if he pays the full balance due within a year. If he doesn't, the interest rate on the balance he owes can jump from nothing to as high as 21 percent. (Remember that in chapter 2, which covers debt, Deena Katz, the financial adviser, warned about store credit cards because of their generally high interest rates.)

Hamman, however, said there is no question that he will pay the balance in full and avoid any charges. Once he sells the house, he will use the proceeds from the sale to pay off the credit cards. "This is basically a bridge loan," he explained. "If I don't sell the house before the year is up on the credit card deals, I'll use a line of credit from my Miami house to repay them because the interest would be much less. I wouldn't have done this if I didn't know that I had an alternative way of paying the cards off. I'm not about to pay twenty-one percent interest." (Interestingly, when Hamman got his first bill from Lowe's, it showed that most of his new charges were subject to interest. He called the company, and the matter was quickly resolved in his favor. "It just goes to show," he said, "how important it is to pay attention to the details of your bill.")

Hamman is one of a growing number of consumers who have learned to win at the credit card game by using plastic to their advantage. It is, however, a game fraught with financial danger; slipups and yielding to temptations can land you in big trouble. You must be disciplined and attentive. Unfortunately, a lot of people aren't, and that is why so many financial advisers counsel against using credit cards.

The problem is that credit cards, like cars, are essential in our modern lives. Without a credit card, it can be difficult—in some cases impossible—to rent a car; hotels are often downright surly to cash customers; and if you want to get intimate with airport security personnel, pay cash for an airline ticket. Credit cards also provide a certain amount of legal protection if a product doesn't live up to its claims, and you're protected by law from all but fifty dollars in losses if your credit card is stolen. Unless you're drowning in debt and there is no other way out, canceling or cutting up your credit cards isn't necessarily to your advantage; that would be like giving up driving because you're buying cars that are too expensive. The best way to play the credit card game: make a Herculean effort to pay the balances and then exercise discipline so that you control the cards rather than the other way around.

SIDESTEPPING THE PLASTIC TRAP

By the time Arkansas native Curtis Arnold had graduated from college in 1962 and began graduate studies in business at the University of Texas at Dallas, he was $45,000 in debt to credit card companies. "I was never late on my payments," he recalled. "But I was making minimum payments and barely keeping my head above water. The stress was indescribable; my self-worth was tied up in this debt. I wondered how it happened. I thought I had used these cards for necessities, not frivolous things."

Arnold's experience with credit card debt, and his eventual escape from it, led him to launch a consumer-oriented credit card Web site in 1998 that has become one of the most popular and useful online sources for credit card information. "I struggled and educated myself and learned about interest rates," he said. "Like so many people out there, especially students, I just didn't have a clue at first. I went through the process of learning about credit cards and how they work. I started transferring balances and taking advantage of low introductory rate offers. I also got a home equity loan, which helped pay down my debt. I learned that while I thought I had been using these credit cards for necessities, the definition of a necessity in a rich society like ours is a lot different from someone, say, in a developing country. When you get down to it, necessities are food, clothing, and shelter. I realized that I could have trimmed a lot of corners that I didn't. I just didn't realize what I was doing. I justified my spending by thinking that when I got out of school I would have a six-figure income waiting for me, so my problems were only temporary. I was in graduate school studying international business; I got caught up in the fast-lane mentality. It was also an ego thing to think that credit card companies had such faith in me, as an up-and-coming entrepreneur, that they were willing to give me credit." Now he travels to college campuses to speak to students and warn them of the dangers of credit card debt.

Arnold started U.S. Citizens for Fair Credit Card Terms in 1998; the company operates the Web site www.cardratings.com. Although the site accepts advertising from credit card companies and banks, it is independent; its reviews of cards are based on impartial, objective data. The site also has an agreement with and a link to www.bankrate.com, a highly regarded site which provides a broad range of information for consumers on all kinds of loans and financial products, including credit cards. There are, of course, lots of other Web sites that deal with credit cards; www.cardratings.com has links to many of them.

There is a mother lode of information on credit cards and how to deal with them at www.cardratings.com. Both www.cardratings .com and www.bankrate.com feature articles on such topics as "20 Sneaky Credit Card Tricks," "Reading the Credit Card Fine Print," and "Protecting Your Credit Following ID Theft: A Step-by-Step Plan of Action." Arnold's site reviews and rates credits cards by categories like lowest interest rate, best rewards program, and best cash rebates. One of its most popular features is a section of reviews by consumers—more than 10,000 reviews sorted by credit card type—and the site also provides lists of the best and worst credit cards. The reviews are written by card users and name names, often in sharply pointed ways that reflect the frustrating experience many people have with credit cards and credit card companies. "People, beware of thieves like this one!" is not an unusual comment on the cards that make the least-favored list. "Customer service is top-notch," writes another consumer of the most favored card. There's also a free monthly newsletter that visitors to the site can request to receive via e-mail.

"AN INCREDIBLE FINANCIAL TOOL"

Arnold stresses the importance of credit cards for families today. "They are necessary in our society," he said. "It's hard to function without one. But if you're an aware consumer and educate yourself about credit cards, they can be an incredible financial tool that you can use to your benefit. Of course, there's the potential for financial problems, but if you're smart you can use a card responsibly—and to your favor."

While Arnold agrees with the conventional wisdom of paying credit card balances in full each month to avoid interest and fees, he does allow for one exception: low or zero percent introductory offers like the kind that Henry Hamman used to finance work on his home in Colorado. "You can use credit cards to creatively finance almost any type of purchase," he said. "So taking advantage of low or zero percent introductory-rate offers is an exception when I think it's smart to carry a balance."

Arnold and his wife, in fact, recently charged the purchase of a year-old minivan on their Discover card. "You might think this was stupid, that we were breaking every rule in the book," he said. He explained, however, that the best rate he could get on a car loan was 5.5 percent. So after charging the car on his Discover card, he turned around the next day and transferred the balance to a credit card that was offering zero percent interest for a year on balance transfers. When the year is up, he plans to pay off the balance or transfer it to another card offering zero percent. "You have to plan ahead," he stressed. "You have to know you can pay the balance by the end of the year, or keep your credit up so you'll get more balance transfer offers. I'm sure if I don't pay the car off in a year, there'll be another offer. We did the same thing with our wedding expenses two years ago. We used credit card checks that were treated as a balance transfer. We got zero percent on that deal for a year too." Arnold warned, however, against assuming all credit card checks will be treated the same way; they can carry high fees and charges: "If you use a credit card check, make sure it's treated as a balance transfer, not a cash advance. Always avoid cash advances like the plague." He also cautioned, "Read the fine print on balance transfers to see if there are any onetime fees; you can tolerate them if they are small and you're getting zero interest for a year. If you're going to do this, shoot for a time span of six months or a year for the offer. It's too much trouble otherwise." Not all car dealers, by the way, will accept credit cards for an auto purchase because they must pay a percentage of the sale as a fee to the credit card company, but Arnold's tactic can help with some major expenses.

Playing the credit card game is creative and nontraditional, but Arnold believes it is done a lot more than people realize. "Many small businesses start out by financing their operations with credit cards," he said. "But a lot of people are unaware they can do this; they don't understand the balance transfer process. It's a game; if you're going to play it, play it to win."

For most people, he recommends a maximum of two or three credit cards. "But if you're in the balance transfer game, it can be to your benefit to have multiple cards because it gives you more options. You can call one of the card companies and offer them your business if they give you a balance transfer deal like zero interest for a certain time. It's all about consumer empowerment and being savvy. That's what I preach, and that's what our Web site is all about." What this means is that you should accept the financial products—the credit cards—that you can use to your advantage rather than falling for advertising hype and accepting cards that mainly benefit credit card companies.

Arnold concedes there is so much information on www.cardratings .com that the site, which is updated monthly, can be a bit confusing at first, but don't let the format stop you from mining the riches.

KNOW THE SCORE

Arnold and other credit card experts stress the importance of keeping track of your credit history and rating, especially your "credit score," a three-digit number that has rapidly become the gold standard for determining how much credit you can qualify for. Once you know your credit profile, you should work to improve it. Another reason to know your credit history is that one in four credit reports contains errors. You can only correct the errors if you know about them. Because of a ruling by the Federal Trade Commission, by September 1, 2005, every American will be able to get a free credit report once a year from the three major credit reporting agencies, Equifax, TransUnion, and Experian. Until then, a credit report can cost between twenty and seventy-five dollars.

Basically, your credit score is a number ranging from 300 to 850 generated by a mathematical formula based on information in your credit report. The score is considered a highly accurate prediction of how likely you are to pay your bills: the higher the number, the better your credit; the better your credit, the lower your interest rates will be. There are a few different formulas, but the score most commonly used by lenders and credit bureaus is known as a FICO because it was developed by the Fair Isaac Corporation in California during the 1980s. Here are the factors that make up your FICO credit score:

- Payment history on various debt, including credit cards, mortgages, and other loans. (35 percent of your score).
- Outstanding debt (30 percent of your score). How much do you owe, and how much of your available credit are you using? It's considered best if your credit card balances are not more than 30 percent of their limits. Maxed-out credit cards lower your score.

- Length of time you've had credit (15 percent of your score).
- Credit inquiries on your report (10 percent of your score). Applying for too much credit can lower your score because it may indicate some kind of financial trouble.
- Credit mix, that is, the kinds of credit you have (10 percent of your score).

As Arnold pointed out, you can improve your credit score once you know it—and, of course, once you know the five elements that go into creating it. The first two elements are the easiest for you to improve, and they account for 65 percent of your score.

A detailed explanation of what your credit score means can be found at www.cardratings.com and www.bankrate.com, as well as on a nifty site called www.howstuffworks.com, which also provides do-it-yourself guidance on things from autos to computers to travel.

Www.howstuffworks.com gives an example of how important your credit score can be. On a typical forty-eight-month auto loan, the interest rate can range from a low of around 6 percent to a high of more than 18 percent on the basis of your score alone. If your score is 720 to 850, the rate is set at 6.678 percent; 690 to 719, 7.390 percent; 660 to 689, 9.500 percent; 625 to 659, 12.226 percent; 590 to 624, 16.206 percent; and 500 to 589, 18.598 percent. These rate differences translate into lots of money. If, for instance, you finance a $20,000 car for forty-eight months at 6.678 percent, your monthly payments will be $476; when the loan is finished, you will have paid $2,848 in interest. That same deal, but with a rate of 18.598 percent, would mean a monthly payment of $594 a month. Total interest costs: $8,512! That's almost three times the total interest you would have paid on the lower rate loan. (For these calculations, I used www.banksite.com's online calculators.)

According to www.bankrate.com and Fair Isaac, the percentage of Americans that falls into each of the credit score categories is:

Percentage

499 and below	1
500 to 549	5
550 to 599	7
600 to 649	11
650 to 699	16
700 to 749	20
749 to 799	29
800 and above	11

You should try to be in the top 60 percent, with a credit score above 700.

PAY ATTENTION TO THE DEVIL IN THE DETAILS

The paramount advice for dealing with credit cards is simple: first, pay your balance in full each month unless you are taking advantage of a low or zero percent interest rate on a balance transfer; second, if you have credit card debt, pay it off as quickly as you can. Transferring a balance to another card with little or no interest can make it easier for you to pay your balance down. Remember, your payment history and outstanding debt make up 65 percent of your credit score and are the elements you have most control over.

Further advice from credit card experts and financial advisers seems to boil down to three rules: know the terms, pay attention to fine-print details, and watch out for sneaky tricks. Internet sites like www.cardratings.com and www.bankrate.com can be very helpful in managing these details. For example, the article "15 Must-Know Credit Card Terms" on the www.bankrate.com site clearly defines the terms that credit card companies use. The same site features two of the articles I mentioned earlier, "Reading the Credit Card Fine Print" by Larry Getlen and "20 Sneaky Credit Card Tricks" by Amy C. Fleitas. In addition, on www.cardratings.com, Rebecca

Lindsey can help you make sense of introductory offers with her article "Low Introductory Rate Credit Card Offers Not Always Destined for the Junk Pile." All four articles are required reading.

In general, these articles and experts like Curtis Arnold and financial adviser Deena Katz offer some wise guidelines for managing your credit cards:

- Play hardball with your credit card company. Don't accept higher rates than necessary. Threaten to cancel your card or put your charges on another card if the company doesn't lower a too-high rate, and be prepared to do so, even if your card is with your primary bank or includes a dividend or "miles" plan. Forget brand loyalty; there are thousands of credit cards out there, and competition is fierce. If you're a good customer, a company has every incentive to keep you. In a recent survey, 56 percent of people who called and asked for lower rates got them. My wife and I have a Chase Mastercard; recently the monthly bill showed that the rate had been increased from 7.99 percent to 13.99 percent. I called Chase and was told that there was one of those fine-print notices in a previous bill informing me of the increases—as if that made it OK. I simply replied that the new rate was unacceptable and said I would cancel the card if it wasn't lowered. Within seconds, it was returned to 7.99 percent, and I received a credit for the month of extra charges. If at first you don't get any satisfaction, demand to speak to a supervisor.

- Always remember that there is no such thing as a truly fixed-rate credit card, and your credit card company can change the rules of your card—including the interest rate—whenever it wants. Pay attention to those almost-too-small-to-read notices that sometimes show up with your monthly bill, as my wife and I should have done with Chase. They rarely contain good news. State laws that govern credit cards are the laws of the state where the credit card company is *based*, not where the holder lives. That's why big banks—even regional banks—sometimes have their credit card operations in distant states where laws are often less consumer-oriented.

- Know your credit card company's rules on extra charges and avoid them. Never make a late payment, even if it means driving to the bank or using an overnight courier service. That's because some companies will raise your interest rate to as much as 30 percent if you pay late just once, and "late" can mean receiving your payment after 1 P.M. on the day it's due.

- Be careful with cash advances. They usually carry a higher rate than purchases; if you're making payments, the payments usually go first to that portion of your bill with the *lowest* rate. For cash advances, interest almost always begins accruing immediately; there's no window to pay off an interest-free balance within the month as is the case with purchases.

- Consider getting a card from a credit union or local community bank. These institutions can be more customer-friendly, with smaller fees and more flexible rules.

- Match a credit card to your needs. If you carry a balance, look for low rates. If you pay in full each month, consider a rewards-based card even though it might have higher rates.

The www.bankrate.com article by Amy C. Fleitas on card companies' sneaky tricks is worth a close read. What some of these outfits are doing would make a loan shark blush. Here's a sampling from the article:

- *Bait and switch.* You apply for a credit card you have been offered, but don't qualify. The card company instead sends you a different card with different terms, apparently hoping you won't notice. Advice: don't activate it; call the company and cancel the account.

- *Musical address.* Credit card companies sometimes change the post office boxes they use for payments. If you send your payment to the wrong box number, it may be lost for enough time to make your payment late—making you responsible for a late fee and open to having your rate increased. Solution: always use the envelope provided with your statement or make your payment online.

- *Increasing the rate based on other accounts.* Your credit card company may check your credit report periodically and use any late payments—on an auto loan, say—as an excuse to raise your rate, even though the late payments may be totally unrelated to your credit card. Solution: avoid any late payments and drop the offending credit card company for another.

- *Setting low minimum payments.* It can take a long, long time to pay off your balance if you only pay the monthly minimum, which is usually 2 percent of the outstanding balance. If your balance is $5,000, your rate is 11 percent, and you make a minimum 2 percent payment each month ($100 the first month, $98.92 the second month, and so on), it will take 279 months, or more than twenty-three years, to pay off the balance. You will have spent almost $4,000 in interest during that time. If, however, you make a fixed payment of $200 a month, you will pay off the balance in twenty-nine months, or less than two and a half years, and the interest you pay will be a bit more than $700. Even if you just maintained the first month's minimum payment of $100, you would pay the balance off in sixty-eight months, or about five and a half years; interest would be $1,719.19 This is surely a no-brainer. Www.bankrate.com has an online calculator that allows you to calculate the true cost of making only minimum payments.

Credit cards are simultaneously one of the biggest curses and one of the blessings of our modern financial life. They can be a fast road to anguish and bankruptcy for the unwary. Yet they—and their cousin, the ATM card—make our lives easier in so many ways, especially when we travel. I'm old enough to remember a time when you could be in real trouble if you got stuck in some distant spot without cash. I can also remember when you had to make sure you had cash on hand for the weekend, when the banks were closed.

Perhaps the best feature of credit cards is the safety net they provide for emergencies. The problem lies in not having a cash cushion to pay the credit card balance once the emergency is past. That is one of the most common ways for people to allow credit card spending to get out of control, as Stacia Ragolia, the editor of *The Frugal Woman's Guide to a Rich Life,* pointed out in chapter 4.

A credit card can be a dangerous product. It must be handled with care.

9

Retirement: Relax a Little

We should be trying to pay for a time when, later in life,
we have to rely solely on our own resources.
—DEENA KATZ, FINANCIAL ADVISER AND PLANNER

Many of us feel financially stretched from paycheck to paycheck. This is made even worse by the fact that we are now, more than in a generation or two, increasingly responsible for supporting ourselves during retirement. Indeed, one of the most important motivations for adopting the expense-cutting lifestyle advocated by this book is to be able to put money aside for retirement, for that time when you can no longer work and have only your own resources to fall back on.

Granted, the prospect of your financial future and retirement can be scary. It is, however, made more frightening than it needs to be. To start with, the widely accepted projections from the mutual fund industry and Wall Street that you need 70 to 80 percent of your preretirement income to retire are exaggerated, designed as still more advertising bait to lure customers to buy financial products. In addition, such projections are flawed because they are based on *preretirement income* rather than *postretirement expenses*.

Except for health costs, most people's expenses drop sharply when they retire, especially if they can relocate to a cheaper area of the country or move to a smaller house close to home. You may wind up living mortgage-free because you have accrued enough equity in your home to pay cash for a less expensive house; you may even have money left over to produce income or pay for health insurance if you need it. Keep in mind the Georgia State University study that I mentioned at the end of chapter 2: your retirement nest egg can be reduced by $25,000 for each $1,000 of annual income you don't need to replace when you retire.

So relax a bit. Saving for retirement is important, but you can retire very nicely without a $1-million nest egg. I began to realize several years ago that mutual fund estimates were out of kilter while traveling from the New York City area to visit friends and relatives in the Midwest and South. I was struck by how well they were living on relatively small incomes, at least compared with people in places like New York and California. A big factor, of course, is the relative cost of housing, as we saw in chapter 3. The cost of housing, in fact, is one of the two most important determinants of a successful retirement. The other is health insurance. Many of the additional ways to cut expenses and increase income are valid whether you're working and saving for retirement, getting ready to retire, or already retired. The key is to learn to live *slightly* beneath your means. (If you want more details, my first book, *Retire on Less Than You Think*, discusses the issues facing people near or at retirement age right now. While written primarily for that older group, it nonetheless contains much information helpful to people in their thirties and forties as they plan for retirement.)

HEALTH INSURANCE

While the prospects for having a secure, comprehensive plan for health insurance during retirement are mixed, there are currently several ways to manage these expenses. If you're less than sixty-five years old (and thus not eligible for Medicare), you should not even think of trying to retire without a plan for health coverage. One serious illness could put you on the welfare rolls. Only about 30 percent of employers offer any retirement health benefits, and that percentage is shrinking as health-care costs climb. Don't assume because your employer offers a retiree health plan now that you will be able to take advantage of this benefit by the time you want or need to retire. Thanks to some federal laws, however, individuals can now get guaranteed coverage until they are sixty-five through the COBRA and HIPAA programs; presumably these programs will be around for a long time, although the current health insurance crisis could force some rapid changes if it worsens, as expected. Although COBRA and HIPAA can be more expensive than buying an individual policy in many states, generally the programs offer advantages over individual policies: you cannot be denied coverage for preexisting conditions; there are no waiting periods; and if you do get sick, you can't be singled out for a rate increase. As discussed in chapter 5, however, there are a few states with guaranteed-issue laws and community ratings, but health insurance policies in those states are relatively expensive. The bottom line: unless you're very healthy and have no preexisting conditions, COBRA and HIPAA provide sure paths to guaranteed coverage and stable rates until you're eligible for Medicare.

COBRA, or the Consolidated Omnibus Budget Reconciliation Act, allows you to continue your employee health insurance benefits at your own expense plus a small administrative fee for eighteen months after you leave your job. That period can be thirty-six months for your spouse if you are eligible for Medicare when you retire but he or she is not. Your spouse is also eligible for thirty-six months if you die or divorce. You must work for a company with twenty or more employees and not have other insurance or be eligible for Medicare. You can get COBRA even if you have been laid off or fired for any reason other than gross misconduct; you must apply within sixty days of your termination date. One warning: if you are going to move, make sure your COBRA plan offers coverage where you're going. For example, if you're in an employer-sponsored HMO, that coverage can be limited and may not be available in another state or area. You might want to switch to traditional coverage during an enrollment period a year or so before you retire—assuming your company or plans will allow it. Otherwise, you could be forced to return to your original location for any care other than emergencies.

Once you have exhausted COBRA coverage, you can take advantage of another federal law called HIPAA, or the Health Insurance Portability and Accountability Act. This means you are eligible for HIPAA plans in every state. Insurers operating in each state must offer two HIPAA-eligible plans, one that is basic and one with broader benefits. These plans cannot differ greatly from other plans an insurer offers. Because insurers must accept all applicants, these policies are expensive. Again, you are guaranteed the coverage without waiting periods and regardless of preexisting conditions. Plus, you can't be singled out for a rate increase. You must apply for HIPAA coverage within sixty-three days of exhausting your CO-BRA coverage, or you lose the right to do so.

Retire on Less Than You Think has an entire chapter on the details of maintaining health coverage when you retire, including some possibilities not included here like short-term and student insurance. The eHealthInsurance Web site (www.ehealthinsurance .com), where you can browse prices anonymously or call a toll-free number for assistance, can also be helpful.

Medicare

Many of the headlines and television teasers about the trustees' annual Medicare report for 2003, issued along with the Social Security report on March 23, 2004, were downright scary: "Medicare Headed Toward Bankruptcy," "Report Predicts Bankruptcy for Medicare by 2019," and "Medicare Could Go Broke by 2019."

The problem is they weren't true. Or, to be more precise, such dire warnings were a "distortion and a disservice" and "totally inaccurate," according to Robert M. Hayes, president of the Medicare Rights Center, a nonprofit organization that helps people with Medicare problems. John L. Palmer, one of two appointed public trustees for Social Security and Medicare, called it "wrong to say Medicare will go broke," adding that the situation was "not as dire as headlines would have you believe."

I guess it all depends on your definition of broke.

What the Medicare trustees said was that by 2019—seven years sooner than was expected in 2003—the hospital insurance trust fund is projected to exhaust its surplus. But because the fund gets its money from the Medicare payroll tax, which would continue, the fund would still be able to pay 80 percent of its bills. This hospital fund, known as Part A, accounts for 56 percent of the Medicare program's spending. Part B, which pays for doctor bills and other outpatient services, gets 25 percent of its money from premiums paid by beneficiaries and 75 percent from general tax revenues. It would not be affected by the depletion of the hospital fund's surplus.

What this all boils down to is a projection that by 2019 Medicare may not be able to pay 20 percent of a 56 percent chunk of its bills without some extra money from somewhere. That represents an overall shortfall of about 11 percent for all Medicare spending combined. If this is a definition of broke, a lot of families, companies, and governments fall into that category.

Another problem is that economic projections like these don't have a great track record, even for the short term. (Consider the inaccurate estimates of federal budget surpluses and deficits over the last five years.) "Medicare projections are based on anticipated increases in medical costs, which are very unreliable because of things like advances in technology," Hayes said. He also pointed out that the 56 percent of Medicare spending for hospitals is shrinking because of new medicines and technologies that are keeping people out of hospitals or shortening their stays. "The whole focus of the new prescription drug program is to treat more people pharmaceutically so they may not need hospital care. Less high blood pressure and fewer heart attacks mean less hospitalization." Palmer, who is also an economist and professor at Syracuse University, agreed that "there is certainly a high decree of uncertainty attached to any long-term projections of medical costs."

Hayes attributed the lost ground in the Medicare trustees' report for 2003 to the weak economy as well as rising health-care costs. "This has much to do with the number of people who are jobless and not paying taxes or are marginally employed off the books and not paying taxes," he said. (The total Medicare tax is 2.9 percent, half paid by the employee and half by the employer; unlike Social Security, the Medicare tax applies to all earnings.)

Efforts to increasingly turn Medicare over to private health maintenance organizations and managed-care companies are also running up costs. Medicare's administrative costs run about 2 percent, whereas for private insurance it's 12 to 18 percent because of expenses like advertising, executive salaries, and lobbying. "HMOs and managed-care companies can't compete with Medicare," Hayes said. "Their Medicare plans run about 10 percent more than traditional fee-for-service Medicare. One reason for this is that because Medicare is so big, insurers can't match it on economies of scale."

Hayes contends that because of this cost difference, the political battle over Medicare has turned the liberal-conservative argument on its head: "You normally think of conservatives as being concerned about keeping federal spending down. So they are saying we don't have enough money for a comprehensive drug benefit; but at the same time they are pushing these wildly expensive HMOs. A significant piece of Medicare expense is the high costs of privatization. The conservatives, by pushing privatization, end up calling for spending more, not less, money. But if you say often enough that privatization saves money, people buy it. The mainstream press has not covered this very clearly."

Despite the political push and pull over Medicare, it remains immensely popular. Owing to its popularity, it's likely to be around in some form or another for a long time and remain a program you can at least partly count on in your retirement planning. Because of continuing budget squeezes and cutbacks, however, you may increasingly need to consider buying supplemental coverage. Of course, Medicare helps you save in a way you might not have considered: it pays, or will pay, your parents' medical bills. This means you won't have to sacrifice your savings or take out a second mortgage on your house if your mother or father, or both, suffer an expensive illness. This was not the case prior to the enactment of Medicare in 1965.

SOCIAL SECURITY

Many American are convinced that the Social Security system is gong broke. *Looming insolvency* is the term most often used in the media to describe the system's purported plight. Poll after poll reflects this concern; many younger people say they expect they will never receive any Social Security benefits despite years of paying the tax. Efforts are under way to "rescue" the system by privatization, which would allow individuals to invest some amount of their Social Security taxes in the stock market.

Well, you can stop worrying. None of these dire predictions is even remotely likely. Privatization might well do more harm than good by creating a system of winners and losers, trading a sure thing for a stock market bet. So-called reform of Social Security increasingly looks like a solution in search of a problem. Even under relatively modest economic forecasts, Social Security is rock-solid until at least 2042. With some minimal changes, it will be fine until 2075 or so and perhaps until the end of the century. That's assuming future economic growth is just half the annual average of about 3.5 percent over the last seventy-five years.

Why all the fuss? Hidden agendas, on all sides. Many conservatives and others who are ideologically opposed to the whole concept of government-sponsored social insurance would like to at least partly privatize the system. They have been joined in the fight by

Wall Street, whose executives and brokers are more than a little excited about the fees and commissions that would be generated from privatization.

Proponents of privatization don't like to be reminded that, as we have seen in recent years, stocks can go up as well as down. The Center for Economic and Policy Research (www.cepr.net) in Washington, D.C., has calculated that if the most modest of the various privatization plans had been put into effect at the beginning of 1988, by November 1, 2002, the Social Security system would have lost $45 billion. Also, Social Security is a pay-as-you-go system: today's retirees are supported by today's workers. The surplus in the trust fund is there to handle the bulge in the retiree population that will occur when large numbers of baby boomers soon begin to retire. Partial privatization would take up to a third of current revenues and put the money into private accounts. How would this money—upwards of $200 billion a year—be replaced so that current benefits could be paid? The government could increase taxes, take on more debt, or cut benefits—all unpleasant solutions to a problem that didn't need to be created in the first place.

It's not just conservatives who are exaggerating Social Security's problems. The Democrats try to score points by depicting themselves as the great saviors of Social Security. During his presidency Bill Clinton, for example, exhorted Congress to use the budget surplus to "save" Social Security. The Republicans aren't about to cry foul and say the system doesn't need saving. If they do, there goes their argument for privatization.

The truth is, Social Security ought not to be a political issue; people should pay more attention to the annual report of the trustees of Social Security and Medicare (www.ssa.gov) and less attention to Washington politicians and their hidden agendas. The Social Security report for 2003 was essentially the same as the 2002 report. It projects that in 2018, the system will have to dip into the trust fund surplus to pay baby-boomer benefits, which is what the extra money is there for, and the surplus will be exhausted by 2042. Even then, without any changes and under modest economic projections, the system could still pay 73 percent of benefits. Minor changes made now, including increasing the amount of income subject to Social Security tax—in other words, collecting the tax on income above the current (2004) cap of $87,900 and thereby making it somewhat less regressive—could help ensure that there is still a surplus in the trust fund when 2042 rolls around. The longer we wait, the more the fix will cost—assuming, of course, the projections pan out. If the past is any guide, economic growth may be greater than projected, and that alone could solve much of the problem. Palmer, the public trustee for Social Security and Medicare, concedes there is a "tremendous amount of uncertainty" in these long-term projections.

(In June 2004, the nonpartisan Congressional Budget Office estimated that the surplus in the trust fund actually won't be exhausted until 2052, a decade later than the trustees' projection. Much of the media, however, reported this new date as the year when Social Security will "go bankrupt." That, of course, is not true; only the surplus will be exhausted, and the pension system will still be able to pay most benefits from money coming in, just as in the 2042 projection. That's a long way from "bankrupt.")

The Social Security trust fund and its surplus, which is invested in government securities, has become a political football because it is often misunderstood by the public. That the trust fund is expected to start redeeming these securities in 2018 to help pay benefits is often cited by critics as a big problem for Social Security because the payout will come from the Treasury.

That's not Social Security's problem. It's a fiscal problem for the government, which has spent and is spending workers' money that was invested in the securities. Through 2003, the fund contained a surplus of $1.5 trillion in bonds, which earns 6 percent interest a year—or $84.9 billion in 2003. If Congress doesn't want to repay the money, it shouldn't have borrowed it in the first place. To see the redemption of those bonds as a problem for the Social Security system is akin to borrowing money from a bank and then, when the debt comes due, declaring it the bank's problem. Palmer agreed with that assessment but noted that the exhaustion of the trust fund surplus in 2042 would be a Social Security problem. Also, the bonds aren't all going to be cashed in at once. They'll be gradually redeemed by the Social Security Administration as needed over two decades or so, assuming the projections are correct. In past years, the dates when the system is expected to face problems have been extended as economic conditions have improved. That is likely to happen again and again.

Here are some Social Security facts—all explained in greater detail on www.ssa.gov—that you should be clear on as you decide how much money to set aside for retirement.

- The tax you pay for Social Security is 6.2 percent of your income, up to an annual limit that was $87,900 in 2004. Your employer pays another 6.2 percent, for a total of 12.4 percent. If you are self-employed, you must pay the entire 12.4 percent. That annual salary limit for Social Security taxes rises each year based on increases in the national average wage.

- You can take early retirement benefits at sixty-two, but they will be reduced by a percentage that depends on the age at which you are eligible for full benefits, which currently ranges from sixty-five to sixty-seven years old and depends on when you were born. The closer you are to full-benefit age, the less your benefits are reduced. If your full retirement age is sixty-five, and you retire at sixty-two, your monthly benefits will be reduced by about 20 percent; at sixty-three, about 13.3 percent; and at sixty-four, about 6.7 percent. If your full retirement age is sixty-seven, and you retire at sixty-two, your benefits will be lowered by 30 percent; at sixty-three, 25 percent; at sixty-four, 20 percent; at sixty-five, 13.5 percent; and at sixty-six, 6.7 percent. If you want to retire early, you'll have to take this into account.

- Monthly benefits are based on an average of your highest thirty-five years of earnings, which are indexed for inflation to bring them up to current dollar amounts. If you don't have thirty-five years of earnings, zeros are used for each year you lack—which will lower your average and your benefits.
- If you retire early and decide to take a part-time job or freelance on your own, be aware of some short-term limits on earnings that will reduce your Social Security benefits. If you are less than your full retirement age, $1 in benefits will be deducted for each $2 you earn above an annual limit that was $11,640 in 2004. In the year you reach full retirement age, $1 in benefits will be deducted for each $3 you earn above a more generous limit that was $31,080 in 2004. In the month you hit full retirement age, all limits disappear; you can earn as much as you want with no benefit reductions. Obviously, if you plan to work in retirement and will have enough money to live on, you might be better off delaying collecting Social Security benefits until your full retirement age.
- You can collect Social Security benefits if you live abroad. However, you generally cannot have access to Medicare benefits overseas.

Pay particular attention to the annual statement you receive from the Social Security Administration. Make certain, for instance, that all the personal information about you is correct and that your record of earnings accurately reflects all the years you have worked. You can also request a statement anytime from the Social Security Web site.

In addition to your earnings record, the statement shows what your monthly benefits will be at age sixty-two and at your full retirement age, based on your earnings history and the assumption that you continue working until you reach those ages. It also shows how much you would get right now if you were disabled, as well as your family's benefits if you died. You should count on these amounts and base your retirement savings plan on the money you need beyond them.

MAKING RETIREMENT WORK

When you're in your twenties, thirties, and even forties, retirement can seem like only a distant possibility. But it comes quicker than you think, and you don't want to get caught spending the last decade of your career struggling to catch up so you have enough money to retire. Better to think about retirement early on when the savings you put aside for it can be less because they have more time to grow.

Along with saving for retirement, you must plan for where you will live. This can make a huge difference in your finances and how much you need to save for retirement, as we saw in chapter 3. If you live in an expensive, high-tax area, you can dramatically lower your expenses by moving to a cheaper place. If you want to stay put, you may want to move to a smaller house or to a less expensive area that is only a short distance away.

Next, you should make three lists of expenses. The first should be your current, preretirement expenses. The second should be postretirement expenses if you stay in your area, and the third should show expenses if you move to a lower-cost part of the country. The two Web sites mentioned in chapter 3—www.BestPlaces.net and www.RetirementLiving.com—can help you with the third list. The biggest differences you will notice, especially if you elect to move, will be in housing costs, insurance, and taxes. Some expenses, especially those related to work, will disappear altogether no matter where you plan to live. Another expense that will go away: saving for retirement.

Let's look at the example of a person who lives in San Francisco and plans to retire to Jacksonville, on the east coast of Florida. To make it easier to calculate percentages, we'll assume a preretirement salary of $100,000. We'll also assume that the retiree will move from a median-priced home in the San Francisco area that is paid for to a median-priced home in Jacksonville.

First, according to data from www.BestPlaces.net, this person will only need to plan for $51,577 a year to maintain the same standard of living in Jacksonville that he or she had on a $100,000 salary in San Francisco. In other words, it is 48.4 percent cheaper to live in Jacksonville than in San Francisco. That figure assumes a mortgage and work-related expenses. Without those, it's much cheaper still. Yet the financial services industry says this person would need to plan for $70,000 to $80,000 a year to retire!

The median price of a home in San Francisco is $560,500. The median price of a home in Jacksonville is $142,600, *below* the national average of $170,800. That means if our retiree sells his or her San Francisco home and pays a 5 percent real estate broker's fee of $28,025, he or she can plan to walk away with $532,475. If $142,600 of that is used to buy a house in Jacksonville, that means $389,875 is left over. At 6 percent a year, that amount would yield an annual income of $23,393—without ever touching the principal. The property tax rate is higher in Jacksonville than in San Francisco, but the total paid will be much less because of the difference in home values. Other taxes, however, are less. State income tax is 6 percent in California; there is no state income tax in Florida. Sales tax is 8.25 percent in San Francisco, compared with 6.35 percent in Jacksonville. Auto insurance on a midsize sedan is about 35 percent less in Jacksonville than in San Francisco.

Here are some other cost comparisons, using indexes with the national average set at 100. Food and groceries are 117 in San Francisco and 103.4 in Jacksonville; transportation, 142 and 104.8; utilities, 120 and 99.9; health, 148 and 95; and miscellaneous expenses (which make up 30 percent of the cost of living), 137 and 101.

You can plug in your own city choices, using www.BestPlaces.net, and see for yourself the astounding differences in the cost of living in various parts of the United States. You don't have to travel very far from the expensive areas for it to drop sharply. About an hour and a half east of New York City, for instance, is the Allentown-Bethlehem area of Pennsylvania, where it is almost 58 percent cheaper to live, even including a mortgage and work-related expenses, than in New York. You should calculate your retirement savings based on your own plan, not based on the plans of the mutual fund industry.

Www.RetirementLiving.com is helpful for comparing taxes imposed by each state. It also has links to news sources and publications about seniors and retirement. There is a directory of state agencies that deal with aging issues, and visitors to the site can sign up for a free e-mail newsletter. In addition, the site has sections on retirement communities and senior housing, as well as products and services. Keep in mind, though, that those offering housing, services, and products have not been evaluated by the site; they are simply there because they have paid a fee.

Real Freedom: Working It Out

The quickest way to double your money
is to fold it over and put it back in your pocket.

—WILL ROGERS

Earlier in this book, I pointed out that living well while spending less will only pay off if you actually put the savings aside, no matter how small, rather than frittering the money away on little things. The simplest but still the best way to do that is to open a separate savings account at your bank, an account dedicated to your new-found savings. Calculate how much money you cut from your budget, and each week actually put that money in the account. At the end of each month, move the money into a mutual fund or some other investment (remember the Hammonds' beach house) that will pay more than a savings account. Or you could use the money to pay down a credit card balance or to prepay your mortgage. The important thing is that you will have put a savings mechanism and process into motion. Keep it going and watch the savings build—or the debt decline.

Let's now take a hypothetical couple with two school-age children and look at some obvious, easy, and specific ways they can start saving money based on the expert's advice outlined in the previous chapters. What we want to consider are not onetime savings but regular savings that will be a constant source of funds for that dedicated bank account. The numbers we'll use are based on national averages. (You can adjust them to match your own situation.) Let's further assume that our family, headed by Joe and Sue Sample, owns a home and has health insurance through one spouse's job.

CREDIT CARDS

The average American household has credit card debt of at least $8,900. We'll give the Samples a break and assume they have a Visa card with a $6,000 balance that carries an annual percentage rate of 11 percent. They are making the minimum payment of 2 percent of the balance each month or $120. At that pace, it will take 296 months, or almost 25 years, to pay the balance; they will have spent $4,826.04 on interest.

The Samples' first move should be to negotiate a lower rate, or switch to another card that has one, and to pay more than the minimum 2 percent each month. They should be able to do that with some of the money they are going to save elsewhere. If they get their rate lowered to 8 percent—and make no other changes—their bill will be paid in 247 months, or about twenty years, and they will have paid $2,860.38 in interest. If instead of paying the minimum each month ($120 the first month, $118.40 the second month, and so on), they pay a fixed amount equal to just the first month's minimum, the balance will be paid in sixty-two months, or a little more than five years, with interest of only $1,322.77. The Samples will have saved $3,503.27 from the lower rate and the fixed amount equal to the first month's minimum. If they pay $150 a month, the debt is gone in forty-seven months, or less than four years, and the interest is further cut to $1,001.89. If, however, they can pay $200 a month, the balance will be paid off in thirty-four months, or less than three years, and the interest paid will drop to $716.80. We'll return to the Samples' credit card issue after we have looked at some other areas where they can find savings.

THE LITTLE THINGS

The Samples—in fact, most families—should easily be able to save at least $100 a month by economizing on lunches, sodas, movies, clothes, and groceries. Remember, too, that the point isn't to give up anything; it's to pay less by being a more aware and efficient consumer.

INSURANCE

By accepting bigger deductibles—say, $1,000 instead of $500—on their homeowner and auto insurance, the family should be able to save at least $30 a month.

Their life insurance, however, can be a big source of savings if they are paying for whole life. If both Joe and Jane have policies for $200,000—a not unreasonable amount with two young children and a mortgage—they could be paying as much as $5,000 a year, or $416 a month for them. According to *Consumer Reports* magazine, they could get the same amount of term insurance for around $1,200, or $100 a month. The savings: $316 a month.

EDUCATION

Savings are savings, so the Samples should not try to cut back on money they are putting aside for their children's education. Keep in mind, however, that like the Hammonds, they may wind up not needing all of it for its intended purpose. That's OK. It can shift to retirement savings. The point is, don't try to save money by cutting back on savings. An exception would be if you are saving so much that it forces you to go into debt for living expenses—especially if the interest rate on the debt is higher than the rate the savings are earning.

AUTOMOBILE

The Samples need a new car. They have been looking at a minivan that will cost $28,000. Based on their joint credit score, they can finance it for five years at 5.5 percent with a 10 percent down payment. Their monthly payments on the balance will be $481.35, and the interest they must pay will total $3,680.96.

Now let's see what happens if they take the experts' advice and buy a late-model car that is coming off lease. The Samples could probably get a three-year-old version of the minivan for around $14,000. At that figure, they may be able to finance it for a period of less than five years, but let's still use five years for the sake of comparison. Interest rates are higher for a loan on a used car, so the Samples will likely have to pay 6.5 percent. With 10 percent down, their monthly payments for five years will be $246.53 and the interest will total $2,192.01. The monthly savings on their car payment comes to $234.82. That's a sustainable savings because they can do the same thing each time they need another car.

The Samples had originally planned to make a down payment of $2,800 on a new minivan. What if they went ahead and put that same amount down on the three-year-old vehicle? Their monthly payments would drop to $219.14 from $246.53, and the interest would total $1,948.45 instead of $2,192.01. It's not a big difference, but unless the Samples can invest the extra $1,400 at an interest rate that's greater than 6.5 percent, it may be a good idea to add this money to the down payment. They decide, however, to earmark the money for an emergency fund, which could enable them to pay cash for an unforeseen expense and thus avoid a credit card charge—at an interest rate that, no doubt, would be more than 6.5 percent.

Figure 10

Worksheet: Increasing Income, Finding Savings

	Current weekly costs	New weekly costs	Weekly savings	x 4 =	Monthly savings
The little things					
Groceries					
Dining out during workweek					
Beverages					
Movies, entertainment					
Clothes					
Others					

	Current deductible	New deductible	Current premium	New premium	Monthly savings
Insurance					
Homeowner's					
Auto					
Life					
Other					

	New car loan amount	Used car loan amount	New car loan payment	Used car loan payment	Amount saved monthly
Automobiles					
First car					
Second car					

Your total monthly savings

Figure 10

Worksheet: Eliminating Debt and Saving for the Long Term

	Current card terms	Negotiated new terms	Scenario 1	Scenario 2	Scenario 3
Credit cards: The power of negotiating lower rates, paying more each month					
Interest rate					
Minimum payment					
How long to pay?					
Total interest paid					
Interest expense saved:					

	Monthly savings	Annual savings	Interest rate	Total after: 20 years	30 years
Compounding: How monthly savings add up over time					
Little things			6%		
Insurance			6%		
Automobile			6%		
Subtotal					
Less: Credit card payment			6%		
Total					

ADDING UP THE SAVINGS

With little effort and virtually no sacrifice, our family has managed to cut monthly expenses in three areas:

Little Things	$100.00
Insurance	$346.00
Automobile	$234.82
	————
Total	$680.82

By cutting these expenses, the Samples have basically increased their income by the same amount. Suddenly, they're almost $700 a month richer.

Let's return to the issue of their Visa card. The family can clearly now afford to make a $200 payment and, if they don't make further charges, pay off the entire balance in thirty-four months. The $680.82 in savings listed above does not include reduced interest from making this bigger credit card payment.

That leaves the Sample family with $480.82 to put in their special savings account each month, and they'll probably be able to increase that allotment when their credit card bill is paid. If, however, they maintain just that rate for twenty years, and invest the money at 6 percent, they will have a nest egg of $223,750.11 to supplement their Social Security and pension income. Just as important, along the way they will be building up the cash available to them in case of an emergency. This means they will not have to borrow money or run up a credit card bill for an illness or a home repair. As was pointed out earlier, it's events like these that can get people into financial trouble if they don't have a cushion to fall back on.

In the case of the Samples, I selected obvious and easy areas for savings, and I purposely underestimated the potential savings. The Samples might easily be able to save more, depending on where they live, or if they move to a cheaper area where housing costs and taxes are less. Most families could surely save more on the little things. For a week or two, keep careful track of the amount of money you fritter away on a daily basis and how much money you spend on financial products like credit cards and auto loans that are costing you money rather than saving it for you. You will be amazed at the amount. As you consider your own finances, you will find other ways to save money and discover how these savings compound over time. When you put your mind to it, you can turn painless savings into a small fortune. *Cutting expenses increases income. You can live well on less than you think.*

Resources

ON THE WEB

www.bankrate.com provides consumer information on financial products including mortgages, credit cards, automobile loans, money market accounts, certificates of deposit, checking and ATM fees, home equity loans, and online banking fees. The site also has good online calculators.

www.banksite.com is another good source of online calculators.

www.BestPlaces.net is one of the best sites for comparing housing and cost-of-living data around the United States, as well as data on crime, education, economics, health, and climate. It also has a calculator that allows you to figure out how much income you would need in order to maintain your current lifestyle in another city or region.

www.Bloomberg.com has some good "what if" calculators that allow you to see, among other things, the advantage of prepaying a mortgage. The site is operated by Bloomberg News.

www.cardratings.com will tell you just about anything you need to know about the hundreds of credit cards available. Cards are rated and reviewed by the site and by consumers.

www.cepr.net is the Web site for the Center for Economic Policy Research in Washington, D.C. The center's economists are convinced that we are in the midst of a housing bubble that will soon burst. The site also has a lot of good data on the Social Security debate.

www.ConsumerReports.org is *the* site, although it's not free, for coping with a wide range of consumer issues and questions, including advice on various kinds of insurance.

www.cpfboard.org, the site of the Certified Financial Planner Board of Standards, can tell you if an adviser has been the source of any consumer complaints.

www.Edmunds.com is chock-full of information for those who need to buy a new or used car.

www.ehealthinsurance.com is a big online broker. Here you can buy health insurance or just get the lowdown on what's available in the various states. The company is a major player in new catastrophic health insurance policies that are linked to health savings accounts.

www.healthinsuranceinfo.net is the site for the Georgetown University Health Policy Institute, a source for current information on health insurance in various states.

www.howstuffworks.com is a great site for the just-plain-curious.

www.iVillage.com deals with financial and other issues specifically for women, although some of its material also appeals to men.

www.kbb.com is the Kelley Blue Book site for determining the value of new and used cars.

www.kff.org, which is run by the Kaiser Family Foundation, provides comprehensive health-care data on the states, including differences in the prices of prescription drugs.

www.mathsisfun.com is for people who can't remember the finer points of high school and college math or are trying to come to grips with math terms that often appear in financial data and articles.

www.mortgages.interest.com has comprehensive information on mortgages, as well as good online mortgage calculators.

www.nahu.org is run by the National Association of Health Underwriters. It can help you find an independent insurance broker in your area.

www.naic.org is the site of the National Association of Insurance Commissioners, a group that assists states in dealing with insurance regulations.

www.napfa.org, the site of the National Association of Personal Financial Advisors, can help you select a fee-only adviser in your area.

www.ofheo.gov is the Web site of the Office of Federal Housing Enterprise Oversight, a government agency that, among other things, tracks the changes in home values around the United States.

www.practicalmoneyskills.com is a really good site for basic help on personal finance.

www.Realtor.com is a great site for looking at homes for sale around the country. It's operated by the National Association of Realtors and is an eye-opener to the wide range of prices for comparable homes in the United States.

www.RetirementLiving.com is good for comparing the taxes imposed by each state.

www.ssa.gov is the Web site operated by the Social Security Administration. It provides an enormous amount of information on rules and benefits. Its data are rock-solid and accepted by all sides in the political debate over Social Security's future. You can use the site to request an estimate of your benefits, or you can calculate your own—very important features for people of all ages who are planning and saving for retirement.

OFF THE SHELF

Age Works: What Corporations Must Do to Survive the Graying of the Work Force (Free Press, 2002), by Beverly Goldberg, makes the case for retaining and hiring older workers.

Cities Ranked and Rated: More Than 400 Metropolitan Areas Evaluated in the U.S. and Canada (John Wiley & Sons, 2004), by Bert Sperling and Peter Sander, provides facts and information on more than 400 cities in the United States and 30 in Canada. Sperling also runs the www.BestPlaces.net Web site.

The Frugal Woman's Guide to a Rich Life (Rutledge Hill Press, 2003), edited by Stacia Ragolia, is a compilation of advice from visitors to the www.iVillage.com Web site about leading a simpler life and saving money. It is aimed at women but also appeals to many male readers.

Generations: The History of America's Future, 1584 to 2069 (William Morrow, 1992), by William Strauss and Neil Howe, is vital for understanding generational issues and how they play out in our national history and public policy.

The Great 401(k) Hoax: Why Your Family's Financial Security Is at Risk and What You Can Do About It (Perseus, 2002), by William Wolman and Anne Colamosca, is a scathing attack on the idea, much ballyhooed by Wall Street, that 401(k) plans linking workers' retirement well-being to the stock market are an easy way to amass wealth. The authors remind us why these so-called defined-contribution plans were created to replace traditional defined-benefit pension plans: not to empower or enrich workers but to relieve corporations of the expense and responsibility of funding and maintaining traditional pensions that are protected and guaranteed under federal law. With 401(k) plans, when employees retire they take their money and that's that. A company has no pesky long-term commitments to retirees, which is great for the corporate bottom line but not necessarily for workers. The authors call for workers to have unrestricted investment choices for their 401(k) plans and for company matches to be in cash, not stock (remember Enron?).

Harvard Schmarvard: Getting Beyond the Ivy League to the College That is Best for You (Three Rivers Press, 2003), by Jay Mathews, takes a contrarian look at prestigious schools and offers solid advice for students who are trying to decide where to apply for college.

How Not to Go Broke at 102!: Achieving Everlasting Wealth (John Wiley & Sons, 2003), by Adriane C. Berg, the radio talk show host, offers guidelines for making the right choices early on to ensure financial security throughout a long and active life.

Rocking the Ages: The Yankelovich Report on Generational Marketing (HarperBusiness, 1997), by J. Walker Smith and Ann Clurman, looks at generational issues from a consumer and marketing point of view.

Social Security: The Phony Crisis (University of Chicago Press, 2001), by Dean Baker and Mark Weisbrot, is a valuable guide for people of all ages who are nervous about or confused over the political discourse on the future of Social Security. The authors make a case against privatization, which they say is promoted by ideologues who have never liked the system and Wall Street brokerage firms eager for huge commissions.

The Two-Income Trap: Why Mothers and Fathers Are Going Broke (Basic Books, 2003), by Elizabeth Warren and Amelia Warren Tyagi, argues that middle-class parents are suffering from an unprecedented and totally unexpected economic meltdown, not necessarily of their own making. The authors call for social and legal solutions, including prohibiting credit card companies from charging grossly unfair interest rates and exposing banks that steer minority customers to higher mortgage rates with an eye to future foreclosures.

Entries in *italics* refer to figures and tables.

Aaron, Henry J., 55
AARP, 83
accidental-death insurance, 85
Age Works (Goldberg), 55, 166
Albany Free School, 2, 3, 4
"Ambition Tax, The," 28–29
Arnold, Curtis, 131–36, 138
assets. *See also* investment
    home as, 21, 31, 59
    long-term-care insurance and, 83–85
    putting money into, other than house,
        30
ATM card, 141
automobile, 116–28
    average per-mile cost, 118
    cost of owning new, *120*, 126–27
    depreciation and expenses during first
        year, 117–21
    getting by with one, 116
    maintenance and repair costs, 117–21,
        123, 126
    true cost to own (TCO), 118–21
automobile, buying, 121–27
    from auto dealer, 121–23
    from broker, 123–24
    on eBay, 3
    late-model used, 117–19, 159
    new, for long haul, 125–27
    new vs. used, 116–18, 119–21
    saving money and, 124–25, 159
automobile finance companies, 79
automobile insurance, xi, 79, 127–28
    collision coverage, 128
    just one car and, 116
    retirement in cheaper area and,
        154
automobile leases, 117
automobile loan, 117–19
    as bad debt, 21
    cost of dealer, 123

cost of interest on, 119
credit score and, 136
low-interest credit card loan vs., 133
saving on payments, 159
reason to take on, 29
automobile-rental insurance, 85

baby boomer generation
    community and, 17–18
    credit card debt and, 25
    debt as weakness of, 19
    defined, 8, 10
    Gen X vs., 14–15
    happiness and, 18
    housing market bubble and, 58
    moving for retirement and, 35
    retirement of, jobs for younger
        generations and, 53–54
    spending of, retirement and,
        10–13
Baker, Dean, 167
balance, credit card, 133, 137
    credit limit and, 135
    low minimum payments and, 140
    transfers, 131, 134, 137
bank debit card, 32
bankrate.com, 23, 132, 136, 137, 139, 163
barter, 6
Bean, Orson, 103–5, 107, 114
Berg, Adriane C., 167
BestPlaces.net, 42–43, 46, 56, 153, 154, 163
Bloomberg.com, 32, 163
bulk purchases, 71
Bureau of Labor Statistics, 43
Burns, Scott, 33
Burtless, Gary, 55
business taxes, 44
Business 2.0 magazine, 54, 56
Butler, Robert N., 9–10, 18
buying clubs, 71

Caddell, Pat, 11
Cambridge Consumer Credit Index survy, 22
cancer insurance, 85
cardratings.com, 132, 134, 136, 137, 163
career
    changing, cost of living and, 35, 47
    short, of Gen X, 16–18
Carter, Jimmy, 11–12
cash, shopping with, 32, 74
cash advances, 139
casualty insurance, 79
Census Bureau, 86
Center for Economic and Policy Reserch (CEPR), 149, 164
Certified Financial Planner Board of Standards (CFP), 80, 164
Chase Investment Services, 105–6
"cherry picking," 92
children
    college education, 103–15
    first having, 16
    life insurance and, 81, 82–83
Chiorini, Matt, 35, 42
cities
    auto insurance and, 127–28, 127
    post-retirement planning and, 153–55
Cities Ranked and Rates (Sperling), 44, 166
cleaning supplies, 69–70
Clinton, Bill, 89, 149
clothing, spending on, 70, 72–73
Clurman, Ann, 8, 167
COBRA (Consolidated Omnibus Budget Reconciliation Act), 93, 96
    early retirement and, 144–45
Colamosca, Anne, 166
College Board, 106
college education
    community, 106
    evaluating, 111
    financial aid and, 110, 111
    later earnings and, 110
    less expensive, 107–9
    loans, 3, 28–29, 114
    number of workers with, 54, 55
    prestige, 109–11, 114
    private, vs. public, 105–11
    saving for children's, 103–15, 158–59
"Coming Job Boom" (Kaihla), 54
community, 17–18
community college, 106
community rating, 91–92, 144
competition, 14
compound interest, 77

compound savings, 75–77, 76
Congressional Budget Office, 150
Constantine, Jay, 90
consumer debt, total unsecured, 21–22
consumerism, resisting mindless, ix, 1, 69–70
Consumer Reports, 79, 85, 86, 164
    auto reports, 125
cooperative investment group, 2
copayments
    HMO, 97
    HSA-eligible plans, 101
    PPO, 98
Costco, 71, 76
cost of living, geographic area and
    area and post-retirement income, 143
    choosing where to live and work, 35–53
    comparing housing, 57–63
    comparing other than housing, 64–67
    executives vs. salespeople, 49
    insurance costs and, 79
    metroplitan areas charts, 36–41
    move to less expensive area and, x–xi
    nurses vs. clerks, 50
    salaries and, 34, 42–43, 46–53
    taxes and, 44
    top job creation areas and, 56
    Web sites and, 42
    white- vs. blue collar salaries and, 48
coupons, grocery, 70–71
credit
    establishing, 30
    length of time, 136
    too easy for people to get, 24
credit cards, 11, 129–41
    advantages vs. disadvantages of, 130–31, 140–41
    as bad debt, defined, 21
    bait-and-switch trick, 139
    balance transfers and, 134
    bills, 3
    calculator, online, 23
    cash advances, 139
    cash purchases vs., 74
    changing rates, credit report and, 140
    department store, 31
    devil in details and, 137–41
    extra charges, rules and, 139
    generations and, 25, 27–28
    importance of avoiding debt, 132
    interest rate increases and, 21, 23–24
    interest rates, 32
    introductory offers, 138
    late payments, 139, 140

local bank or credit union and, 139
loss protection, 85
low-interest promotions, 32, 129–30, 133–34
low-minimum-payment trick, 140
matching, to needs, 139
minimum payments on, 131, 140
musical address changes and, 139–40
negotiating lower rate on, and paying off, 157–58
number of households carrying balances, 22
number to own, 31
paying off, and controlling, 131
paying off, as quickly as possible, 137
paying off, with small savings, 156, 162
pay-off-balance-monthly rule, 31
penalty rates and fees, 23
playing hardball with company, 138
sneaky tricks and, 137
terms, 137
credit card Web site, consumer oriented, 131–32
credit disability insurance, 86
credit history, 135
credit inquiries, number of, 136
credit-life insurance, 86
credit mix, 136
credit reports, errors in, 135
credit score, 135–37, *137*, 159
credit union, 2, 139

Dale, Stacy Berg, 109
Dallas Morning News, 33
day care, cost of, compared, *64–65*
debt, 20–33. *See also* automobile loans; college education; credit cards; mortgages
baby boomers and, 11, 13–14
cautious approach to, 29
college and, 112, 113
cutting bad, 19, 21–22, 30–32
cycle of, ix
generations and, 25–29
good vs. bad, defined, 21
higher interest rates and, 23–24
reasons to avoid and pay off, 29
retirement and bad, 25–26
rule for taking on, 29–30
worksheet for eliminating, *161*
deductibles, on insurance, 79
health, 93–94, 96, 98–99
homeowner and auto, 158
Defense Department, 54

Democrats, 149
depreciation, 118–20, 125–26
disability insurance, 79–81, 86
divorce rates, 14
Dobbins, Gary, 117, 119, 121–24
downsizing, 6, 12, 13, 86

eBay, 73
Edmunds.com, 118–19, 125, 164
eHealthInsurance, 91, 92, 94, 97–101, 145, 164
electricity, 10
emergency
credit card as safety net for, 141
savings to cover, 75, 162
unemployment fund and, 86
employer
bonds with employees unraveling, 9
disability insurance and, 81
health insurance and, 90–93, 95–97
health insurance, after leaving job, 144–45
long-term-care insurance and, 84
Equifax, 135
estate preservation, 84
expenses. *See also* specific types
automobiles and, 116–28
credit cards and, 129–41
education and, 103–15
five areas for cutting, 70–75
geographic area and, 35–53
insurance, 78–102
little things, 68–77, 76, 158
postretirement list for current area, 153
postretirement list for lower-cost area, 153
preretirement list, 153
retirement and, 33, 142–62
savings or income realized from cutting, ix, 6, 19, 33, 156–62
worksheets on cutting, *160–61*
Experian, 135

Families USA, 86, 88
family, 17–18
activities, cutting spending on, 70, 74
federal budget deficit, 16, 31
federal catastrophic health insurance proposal (1972), 89–90
Federal Reserve Board, 21
Federal Trade Commission, 135
fee-for-service Medicare, 147
fee-for-service or indemnity plan, 97

FICO (Fair Isaac Corporation) score, 135–36
"15 Must-Know Credit Card Terms," 137
financial adviser, 80
Fleitas, Amy C., 137, 139
flight insurance, 85
food shopping, 71
401(k) plan, 5, 26, 27, 30, 166–67
Freidlen, David, 127–28
Friedan, Betty, 13
friends, circle of, 14, 17
Frugal Woman's Guide to a Rich Life, The (Ragolia), 69, 141, 166
fuel costs, automobile, 121
furniture, 73

games, 74
generations, 1–19
  retirement, 9, 14–16
  three, compared, 8–10
Generations (Strauss and Howe), 8, 166
Generation X, 1, 2, 6
  "baby boomers" vs., 6, 7
  careers and, 16–18
  college loans and, 28–29
  credit cards and, 27–28
  defined, 8–9
  savings and investing and, 27
  retirement and, 4–5
"Generation X and Their Future Buying Behaviors in the Foodservice Industry" (Hoffichter, Wildes, and Parks), 16
geography, xi. *See also* cost of living
Georgetown University Health Policy Institute, 92, 164
Georgia State University, 33, 143
Getlen, Larry, 137
gifts, 74–75
GI generation, 8, 9, 19, 35
Goldberg, Beverly, 55, 166
graduate school, 28, 113
Great 401(k) Hoax, The (Wolman and Colamosca), 166–67
Great Depression, 19
groceries, 70–71, 76
guaranteed-issue laws, 91, 92, 95, 98–102, 144

Hamman, Henry, 129–30, 133
Hammond family, 111–15, 156
Harvard Schmarvard (Mathews), 108, 167
Hayes, Robert M., 146, 147

health care costs, 31, 88
  by state, 65–67
  uninsured and, 89
health indicators, 88–89
health insurance, 3–4, 79, 86–102
  catastrophic policy, 89–90, 93, 93–97
  COBRA law, 93, 96, 144–45
  community rating and, 91–92
  cost of private, 91
  cost vs. access and, 92–93
  end of jobs-based, 90–93
  fee-for-service or indemnity plan, 97
  guaranteed-issue laws and, 91, 92
  HIPAA and, 93
  HMO plan, 97–102
  HSAs and, 93–97, 98–102
  numbers uninsured, 86–87, 89
  portable, 96
  POS plan, 98
  PPO plan, 98–102
  preexisting conditions, 91, 95, 144
  premiums compared, by state, 97–102
  private individual, 91–92
  retirement and, 143–48
  state laws and, 91–92
  uninsured, by age, 87–88, 88
  uninsured, HSAs and, 100–101
  uninsured, reason for, 95
  uninsured, by state, 87
  universal, 88–90
health insurance companies, 89–90
healthinsuranceinfo.net, 92, 164
health savings accounts (HSAs), 90, 93–102
  defined, 93–94
  dedctibles and, 99–102
  -eligible policies, by state, 98–102
  problems with, 94–95
  workplace and, 95–97
Herbert, Bob, 89
HIPAA (Health Insurance Portability and Accountability Act), 93, 144–45
HMOs (health maintenance organizations)
  COBRA and, 145
  defined, 96–98
  Medicare and, 147
  premiums compared by state, 98–102
Hoffichter, Megan, 16
holiday spending, 70, 74–75
home equity, 26
  rent vs. owning and, 59
  residential vs. asset value and, 31
home equity loan
  danger of adjustable-rate, 24
  to pay down credit card debt, 131

home furnishings and decorating, 70, 73–74
home mortgage, 3
    adjustable-rate, 57–58
    baby boomers and, 11
    college costs and, 112–13
    fixed-rate, 58–59
    generations and, 25
    as good debt, 21
    home insurance and, 79
    living without, xi
    online calculators, 32, 165
    postretirement, 143
    prepaying, 30, 32–33
    refinancing, to pay off credit card, 23–24
    thirty year, as wise strategy, 30
homeowner's insurance, 79
home prices
    appreciation of, asset value and, xi, 13,
        21, 31, 59
    buying cheap, 2–3
    buying first house and, 16
    housing market bubble and, 58
    online Web site data on, 59, 63, 64
    regions and states compared, 43–44, 51,
        57–63, 60–61
    retirement and, 154
household formation, of Gen X, 17
housing
    postretirement costs, 153–54
    postretirement income and region, 143
    renting vs. buying, 58–59
Howe, Neil, 8, 166
How Not to Go Broke at 102! (Berg), 167
howstuffworks.com, 136, 164
Hurley, Robert, 94–95

identity-theft insurance, 85
immigration, 55
income. See also salaries
    alma mater and later, 110
    preretirement, post-retirement expenses
        vs., 142–43
income taxes, 44
    disability insurance and, 81
    home ownership and, 58–59
    HSAs and, 93, 101–2
index funds, 26
infant mortality, 88
inflation, 30–32
    home mortgage and, 58–59
    1970s and, 11, 12
Ingram, Mathew, 22
insurance, 78–102. See also specific types
    auto, xi, 79, 116, 154, 127–28

disability, 79–81
    "given," 78
    health, 86–102
    life, 81–83
    long-term care, 79, 83–85, 96
    not always necessary, 78–80
    postretirement costs of, 153
    savings on, 158
    ten kinds you don't need, 85–86
insurance agent, 80
insurance companies, 79
"intentional" community, 2–7
interest, paying down debt and, 29
interest rates
    auto loan, and credit score, 136
    chart, 24
    credit card, 32, 131, 138–39
    danger of higher, 23–24
    fixed, on good debt, 21
    rising home prices and, 57–58
Internal Revenue Service (IRS), 118. See
        also income tax
International Longevity Center—USA,
    10
international stock index, 26–27
investment
    baby boomers and, 26
    borrowing for, 30
    Gen X and, 15
    as goal, 20
    insurance vs., 80
iVillage.com, 69, 75, 164
Ivy League schools, 107–8, 112–13, 115

Japan, 88
jobless recovery, 12
jobs
    coming boom in, 53–55
    cost of living and where to look for, 35
    identification with, 12–13
    future places for, 56–57
Jones, James, 52
Journal of Restaurant and Foodservice
        Marketing, 16

Kaihla, Paul, 54–55, 56, 57
Kaiser Family Foundation, 65, 164
Kasper, Lynn, 42
Katz, Deena, 24–32, 78–85, 96, 97, 129–30,
    138
Kelley Blue Book, 128, 164
Kiplinger's magazine and Web site, 75
    Retirement Report, 83
Krueger, Alan B., 109–11, 113

L.L. Bean, 72
labor shortage, projected, 54–55
Lauer, Gary, 100–101
Lawler, Patrick, 59
layoffs, 6, 9, 13, 15
    health insurance and, 86, 92–93, 144
life expectancy, 88
life insurance, 79–83, 104
    annual renewable term, 82
    investment vs., 80
    level-premium term, 82
    saving on, with term, 158
    universal life, 82
    variable life, 82
    whole life, 81–82, 158
Lindsey, Rebecca, 137–38
Long, Russell B., 89, 90
long-term care insurance, 79, 83–85,
    96
Los Angeles Times, 105
low-birth-weight babies, 88
lower-income lifestyle, 6
lower-income students, 109–10
"Low Introductory Rate Credic Card Offers
    Not Always Destined for the Junk Pile"
    (Lindsey), 138
lunch, 69, 76

McQuinn, Corey, 1–4, 6, 7
Madison, Indiana, 48–53
managed-care companies, Medicare and,
    147
marriage
    delayed, 16
    long-term care insurance and, 84
    retirement health insurance and,
        144
Mathews, Jay, 108, 167
"mature" generation, 8–10
Medicaid, 84, 89
Medicare, 86, 89, 90, 93, 101, 152
    HMOs vs. fee-for-service, 147
    Part A and B, 146
    prescription drug program, 146–47
    projections, 146–47
    retirement and, 144, 145–48
Medicare payroll tax, 146, 147
Medicare Rights Center, 146
merit scholarships, 112
Merv Griffin Show, The (TV show), 103,
    104
metropolitan statistical areas
    home prices and, 63–64
    twenty top, for jobs, 56–57

middle class
    lacking health insurance, 87, 88
    less-expensive college options, 107–8
Moneygame, 2, 3
Money magazine, 42, 75
mortgage. See home mortgage
mortgage life insurance, 85
movies, 74, 77
Murphy, Maureen, 1–4, 6, 7

National Association of Health
    Underwriters, 102, 165
National Association of Independent
    Colleges and Universities, 106
National Association of Insurance
    Commissioners (NAIC), 83, 165
National Association of Personal Financial
    Advisors (NAPFA), 80, 165
National Association of Realtors, 165
necessities, redefining, 131
neonatal mortality, 88
New York, housing market and, 58
New York State Museum, 3
New York Times, 58, 89, 103, 110

Office of Federal Housing Enterprise
    Oversight (OFHEA), 59, 61, 63, 64, 165
outsourcing, 9, 12, 55

paint, 73
Palmer, John L., 146, 147, 150, 151
Parks, Sara C., 16
payment history, 135
pension
    decline of defined-benefit, 26, 27, 105
    Gen X and, 5
    pressures on, 31
Pollack, Ron, 88
POS (point-of-service) plan, 98
PPO (preferred provider organization), 98
    premiums compared, by state, 98–102
practicalmoneyskills.com, 75, 165
preexisting conditions, 91, 95, 144
prescription drug benefit for Medicare, 93,
    146–47
preventive health care, 94, 95
primary-care physician referrals, 97, 98
property insurance, 79
property taxes, xi, 44, 58, 154
public works projects, 10

Ragolia, Stacia, 69–74, 77, 141, 166
"Reading the Credit Card Fine Print"
    (Getlen), 137

"Ready to Face Tomorrow" (Bean), 103
Reagan, Ronald, 12
Real Simple, 18
recessions, 12, 15
rental market, 59
Republicans, 149
retirement, 142–55
    baby boomers and, 9, 13–15, 27
    Gen X and, 9, 15, 17, 27
    health insurance and, 143–48
    home ownership and, 59
    making it work, 153–55
    Medicare and, 145–48
    nest egg, lowered expenses and, 33,
        142–43
    planning for, 4–5
    planning where you will live, 153–55
    saving for, children's education vs.,
        105–7, 114
    small regular monthly savings and, 162
    Social Security and, 10, 148–53
    tax-sheltered investment for, 30–31
    three lists of expenses for, 153–55
retirement, early
    health insurance and, 93, 144–45
    place for, and cost of living, 35
    Social Security and, 151
RetirementLiving.com, 42, 44, 153, 155,
    165
Retirement Living Information Center, 44
Retire on Less Than You Think, x, xi, 143,
    145
risk management, 78
Rocking the Ages (Smith and Clurman), 8,
    167
Rogers, Will, 156
Roosevelt, Franklin D., 10
Runzheimer International, 64–65, 127
Russell 2000 Index, 26–27

salaries. *See also* income
    cost of living and, 34, 35, 42–43, 46–47
    executives vs. salespeople, *49*
    nurses vs. clerks, *50*
    white- vs. blue-collar, *48*
sales taxes, 44, 154
    automobile purchase and, 118
Sam's Club, 71
Sander, Peter, 166
San Francisco, 58
savings
    baby boomers and, 13
    college education and, 114–15
    effect on, of reducing debt, 29
Gen X and, 15
as goal, 20
insurance spending and, 79
little things and, 69–77, *76*, 156, 158
personal savings rates, 21–22
retirement vs. college and, 105
regular monthly, 157, 161–62
starting, 16
worksheet on finding, *160*
worksheet on long term, *161*
Sharkey, Caroline, 1, 3, 4–5
silent generation, 8, 19
Smart Money magazine, 75
Smith, J. Walker, 8–10, 12, 15–17, 25, 27,
    70, 167
Social Security, 4, 9, 145
    calculating benefits, 152–53
    early retirement and, 151
    full benefit age, 151
    future of, 148–50
    Gen X vs. baby boomers and, 15
    limits on earnings and, 152
    living abroad and, 152
    pressure on, 31
    privatization of, 25–26, 148–49
    trust fund surplus, 149–51
Social Security Administration, 151
    annual statement, 152–53
    payroll tax, 4–5, 150
    Web site, 165
Social Security: The Phony Crisis (Baker
    and Weisbrot), 167
soda, 68–69, 76
Some Came Running (film), 52
spending. *See* expenses
Sperling, Bert, xi, 42–47, 56, 59, 166
sport utility vehicle, 121, *122*
Standard & Poor's 500–Stock Index, 26–27
Starfield, Barbara, 88, 89
state income tax, 154
state insurance departments, 83
states
    credit card laws and, 138–39
    with guaranteed issue and community
        rating, 91–92
    health insurance and early retirement
        and, 144
    HSAs and, 94
    insurance and, 79
    long-term insurance regulations and,
        83
    population without health insurance,
        87
    tax burdens compared, 42, 44, *45–46*

state universities, 108
stock market, 13
  buying on margin, 30
  index funds, 26–27
Strauss, William, 8, 166
Suchak, Bhawin, 1–7

taxes. *See specific types such as* income
  taxes; property taxes; sales taxes; states,
  tax burdens compared
teaching, retirement rate, 55
temporary workers, 9
thrift shops, 73, 74
Toronto Globe and Mail, 22
TransUnion, 135
"20 Sneaky Credit Card Tricks" (Fleitas), 137
Two-Income Trap, The (Warren and Tyagi),
  28, 167
Tyagi, Amelia Warren, 167

unemployment
  health insurance and, 86, 92–93
  prospects for future and, 53–55
unemployment insurance, 86
U.S. Census Bureau, 61
  Divisions, home price rises in, *62–63*
U.S. Citizens for Fair Credit Card Terms,
  132

U.S. Congress, 55, 88, 93
  Social Security trust fund and,
    150–51
  unsecured revolving debt,
    21–22

Viale, Chris, 22, 23, 24, 29

Wall, Peter, 105, 106, 108, 114
Wall Street Journal, 80
warranty repairs, 123
Warren, Elizabeth, 28, 167
Web sites, 163–65
Weisbrot, Mark, 167
Weston, Liz Pulliam, 105
Wetzel, Tom, 44
Wildes, Vivienne J., 16
Wolman, William, 166
women, work and, 13
working families
  lacking health insurance, 87, 88
  parents, 14
work parties, 6
World War II, 15, 19

Yankelovich Partners, 8

yard sales, 74

about the author

FRED BROCK, a former business editor and current contributor to *The New York Times*, is the author of *Retire on Less Than You Think* and holds the R. M. Seaton Professional Journalism chair at Kansas State University. He has also been an editor and reporter covering politics, business, and finance for *The Wall Street Journal*, the *Houston Chronicle*, and the *Louisville Courier-Journal*. He lives in Manhattan, Kansas.

You Can Have a Better Lifestyle
Without a Bigger Paycheck

Learn How in These No-nonsense Guides
from Fred Brock

Retire on Less Than You Think
Available in paperback from Times Books

In this indispensable guide, *New York Times* columnist Fred Brock cuts through the mutual-fund industry hype and Social Security scares to deliver frank and pragmatic advice on retirement planning. The book offers the latest thinking on all the essentials for a smart and secure retirement, from finding untapped asset streams to maximizing health-care coverage. It also includes the critical tools for analyzing your true costs of retirement and a substantial list of national, regional, and online resources.

Live Well on Less Than You Think
Available in paperback from Times Books

Fred Brock challenges conventional financial wisdom again in this smart, down-to-earth primer on financial survival—and prosperity—in today's uncertain economy. Here Brock contests the hype that is driving money decisions during the working years—credit card debt, health-care costs, stagnant wages—and shows readers how to analyze their true costs of living so that they can live debt- and worry-free while enjoying themselves and securing their future.

Learn more about these books by visiting www.henryholt.com.